The Cinemas of Camden

A survey and history
of the cinema buildings
of Camden,
past and present

by Mark Aston

Camden
LEISURE & COMMUNITY

London Borough of Camden
Leisure and Community Services Department
Local Studies and Archives Centre
Holborn Library
32-38 Theobalds Road
London WC1X 8PA
0171 413 6342

First Published 1997
Copyright ©Mark Aston 1997
ISBN 0 901389 88 9

Designed by Ivor Kamlish
Map designed by Russell Bell
Produced by FSH Print and Production Ltd.
Printed in Great Britain.

Cover photograph (front); Palace,
Kentish Town, 1913. Reproduced
by kind permission of the National
Monuments Record.

Cover photograph (back);
Everyman Cinema, Hampstead, 1996.
Taken by the author.

Illustrations

The following organisations have kindly
given their permission for photographs
to be reproduced:

British Film Institute (Stills, Posters and
Designs Collection); 20, 28, 29, 58, 59.
Camden Local Studies and Archive Centre;
1, 2, 3, 4, 9, 15,21, 25(below), 40, 42,
44, 57, 60(right), 72.
Hampstead and Highgate Express; 69.
London Metropolitan Archives; 38(above and
below), 45(above and below), 51(below).
Museum of London (Henry Grant
Collection); 43.
National Monuments Record (RCHME Crown
Copyright); 12, 27(above and below), 30,
36(above and below), 47, 49, 54, 55, 56,
61,63, 64, 65, 66, 67, 68.
Photographs taken by the author; 7, 10, 14,
33, 52, 70, 71,73, 74, 75.

Every effort has been made to contact
copyright owners of the illustrations in this
book. If in any instance this has not proved
possible I offer my apologies to those
concerned.

Acknowledgements

I wish to thank all those who have helped to make this publication possible. A very special thanks to Malcolm Holmes and all my colleagues at the Camden Local Studies and Archives Centre who have given unstinting help and encouragement in the realisation of this project. I would also like to mention the published work of Allen Eyles and Keith Skone whose book "London's West End Cinemas" (Keytone, 1991) initially gave me the idea to produce a Camden-wide cinema survey. Their comprehensive coverage of Camden's Tottenham Court Road and West End cinemas provided the background information for these two areas - although I hope that I have added to their original research. Finally, I would like to thank Des Whyman, Anne Woodward of the National Monuments Record, Paul Collett of Camden Arts Service and Peter Woodford of the Camden History Society for editing and much appreciated guidance.

Contents

Introduction

This brief survey has attempted to record the location and, where possible, the history and everyday running of Camden's former and current picture palaces. Perhaps not as grand in stature or reputation as those in London's Leicester Square and West End, Camden's cinemas have entertained and thrilled many an audience over the years and continue to do so today. This brief history aims not only to record Camden's cathedrals of cinema for posterity but also to enable them to be fondly remembered by their audiences.

Although Camden has also been home, and still is, to a number of independent film societies and small private cinema clubs, these will not form part of this survey. In addition, cinemas on the border of Camden have had to be excluded. However, passing homage must be paid to a few like Kilburn's former Gaumont State and Kingsway's Stoll Theatre. These stood only metres outside Camden and can doubtless be vividly remembered by those who regularly visited the buildings during their glory days.

The boundaries of the London Borough of Camden serve as markers for the area covered. Camden was created in 1965 from the former metropolitan boroughs of Holborn, Hampstead and St Pancras.

Historical background

Beginnings

Even before the modern public cinema was born in Britain in 1896, Camden was no stranger to early projected moving pictures. The Frenchman Louis Daguerre produced painted animated panoramic pictures using moving magic lanterns and presented them to the public at the Diorama in Park Square East, Regent's Park, as early as 1823. The shell of the Diorama can still be seen today.

During the 19th century, a wide range of machinery and ideas were being tried out in attempts to create the illusion of moving pictures. An early cinematograph pioneer and Camden resident (136 Maida Vale) was William Friese-Greene (1855-1921). Friese-Greene also worked at 20 Brook Street, Holborn, in 1890 where he was the first to print a moving picture photographed on

The Royal, Holborn in 1897. One of the first theatres in Camden to show moving pictures.

1

Programme from the Royal dated May 1898.
Edison's Lifesize Pictures thirteenth on the bill.

celluloid. He is now a permanent resident of Camden, being buried at Highgate Cemetery in the north of the borough. However, it was the French Lumiere Brothers who first opened their cinematograph show to the paying public on 21 February 1896 at the Regent Street Polytechnic. This is acknowledged to have been the first time the public had paid for cinema in Britain.

By the time of the Lumieres' show, the Holborn area was fast developing as a centre for film-makers, designers and manufacturers of cinematograph equipment. Perhaps the most famous of these was Robert William Paul (1869-1945), reputed father of British cinematography, whose workshop was located at 44 Hatton Garden during this formative period. Paul's pictures of Derby Day 1896 were screened at London's Alhambra Theatre only 24 hours after the race was run on Epsom Downs. Today a plaque commemorates the site of his Hatton Garden workshop. Robert Paul was not alone in his work. Others in the area included J Wrench and Son of 50 Gray's Inn Road, who produced "Wrench's Cinematograph" in 1897, and Philip Wolff of Southampton Street (now Place), who developed his "Vitaphotoscope" the same year.

Before the turn of the century no buildings were erected solely for the purpose of showing films. Moving pictures were shown in music halls and variety theatres, sharing the bill with live acts. In Camden, one of the earliest theatres showing films was the Royal Theatre, Holborn, at 242-245 High Holborn. In 1898, Edison's life-size moving pictures were a regular feature on the bill. The Royal later became the Holborn Music Hall. Another live theatre showing films before 1900 was the Bedford Theatre, 93 Camden High Street, Camden Town. The earliest films were silent and very short, often lasting less than a minute. When filming, the camera remained static and usually recorded actualities - everyday scenes and events. Other types of buildings were also used. For example, the basement of the Hampstead Drill Hall, now the world-famous Everyman Cinema, was a venue for early screenings around 1899, and the Hampstead YMCA in Willoughby Road exhibited moving pictures from 1901.

Later, film was brought to wider audiences through shop shows and travelling bioscope booths at fairgrounds. Many booths had ornamental carved and gilded facades, often lit by floodlights or banks of single lights. Competition amongst travelling showmen to present the grandest frontage was fierce. These mobile cinemas proved popular at Hampstead Heath's annual fairs. Possibly the first to present film on the Heath was Fred Gray, using a hand-wound Gaumont Pathe

The Bedford Theatre, 1904. It was presenting film around the turn of the century, becoming a full-time cinema during the 1930s.

Biddall's Travelling Electric Show (centre background), Hampstead Heath c.1905.

camera. Other exhibitors who entertained crowds on the Heath included the Queen's Cinematograph and, in 1905, Biddall's Electric Show. Film making had also become more sophisticated and technically advanced. Filmgoers were now given narrative stories, drama and comedy as well as newsreels and documentaries. These films also lasted much longer than the early actualities. Travelling cinemas virtually died out before the start of the First World War (1914-1918), but they were an important part of cinema's evolution, bridging the gap between music hall and early permanent cinema buildings.

Early cinemas

As cinema entertainment became widespread the demand for moving pictures from a predominately working class audience steadily grew. Exhibitors thought it worthwhile to organise film displays in their own right and, as a result, Britain's first permanent cinemas were established. Much of the time these early picture palaces were buildings converted from existing theatres, music halls, shops and public premises. The borough's first permanent building devoted solely to film was the Dara in Camden Town. It was established in around 1908 in a converted Victorian public hall. A nearby bakery in Camden High Street was also converted to a cinema in 1909, becoming the Electric Theatre - better known later as the Camden Plaza cinema. The Kilburn Picture Palace began life as the Kilburn Theatre Royal, also converting to film in 1909.

The Cinematograph Act of 1909 forced public cinemas to become licensed by their local authority as a safeguard against the fire risk associated with inflammable film stock. Although some very early cinemas failed to meet licensing requirements, there was then a nationwide growth in the opening of new picture houses, many purpose-built. Picture palaces now offered many refinements, including carpets, soft lights, professional musical accompaniment (often featuring orchestras as well as solo pianists) and usherettes. All this for a low price of admission!

One of the earliest purpose-built cinemas in Camden was the Majestic Picturedrome in Tottenham Court Road, opened in 1912. The following year the Maida Vale Picture Palace, Kentish Town's Palace cinema and the Hampstead Picture Playhouse were built and opened. This last named cinema is still with us today as the ABC, Hampstead. Perhaps the most impressive was the Grange in Kilburn. Claimed to be Britain's first "super-cinema" and certainly one of Europe's largest with a seating capacity of 2028, the Grange opened in 1914. Its design broke away from traditional theatre design towards a totally new approach.

Despite the obvious popularity of cinema, a large number of early cinemas closed during the First World War, even more than in the 1950s and 1960s. This was partly because of the amount of competition but also because of the increasing expense of securing US-made films favoured by audiences and the heavy government cinema tax introduced in 1916. Camden's casualties included the Hampstead Picture Palace, the Kilburn Electric Palace, the Lismore in Gospel Oak and the Fitzroy Picture Palace in Charlotte Street.

Inter-war period and the golden age of British cinema

Although far fewer new cinemas opened than before the First World War, the 1920s still witnessed the appearance of a number of conversions or purpose-built cinemas. Many of these incorporated new designs and increased seating. In 1920 the King's Cross Cinema opened in Pentonville Road and in 1921 the Victory opened in the heart of Holborn. Both were scheduled to open a number of years earlier but a wartime ban on the opening of new places of amusement imposed delays. The most unusual building conversion in Camden's cinematic history came at this time. In May 1924, the Tolmers Square Congregational Church, built in the 1860s, became the Tolmer cinema. For the first 4 years of its existence it still sported the original church spire, making a night out at the pictures a truly spiritual experience! In contrast, the decade also saw the Dominion Theatre open in Tottenham Court Road. Although built as a live theatre, the huge 2835 seat Dominion was soon to convert to cinema. With the introduction of talkies at the end of the 1920s, renewed and increased interest in cinema was witnessed nationally.

The 1930s became widely known as the golden age of British cinema. During this decade the nation saw its greatest number of prestigious cinemas built, as well as many new conversions from live theatre to cinema. Amongst those leading the field in new design and direction was Oscar Deutsch, founder of the Odeon cinema chain. In Hampstead, the Odeon at Haverstock Hill opened in 1934 followed 3 years later by the Odeon, Swiss Cottage - which still survives. Other super-cinemas erected at this time were the Forum, Kentish Town (1934), the Paramount in Tottenham Court Road (1936) and the Gaumont, Regent's Park (1937). Cinema conversions in Camden were also common. The Regent Theatre, King's Cross converted in 1932, and the Everyman Theatre became the Everyman Cinema in 1933. The same year, Camden Town's Bedford Theatre also became a cinema for the remainder of the decade.

Additional features associated with the new super-cinemas were the introduction of mighty cinema organs and lavish stage shows to accompany film programmes. Audiences could enjoy pre-film organ music played on instruments such as the Compton or the Wurlitzer. The organ and organist often appeared whilst playing from below ground or stage and exhibitors claimed the organ could imitate every instrument in an orchestra. Live stage shows were also popular. Tottenham Court Road's Paramount cinema boasted a show that incorporated 76 artists!

For the first few weeks of the Second World War (1939-1945) cinemas closed as a safety precaution against the threat of air-raids. Authorities believed it was dangerous to have large numbers of people under one roof. Soon though the ban was lifted and patrons were warned of imminent raids via an on-screen message or staff announcement. Nevertheless, some cinemas remained closed temporarily and some closed permanently. Temporary closures included Hampstead's Everyman and Picture Playhouse. Others were closed by bombing, for instance the Haverstock Hill Odeon, which was closed from November 1940 until 1954. Other permanent casualties included the Bloomsbury Super (formerly Victory), the Maida Vale Picture House and the Embassy and Sphere cinemas of Tottenham Court Road. Film-going was still extremely popular during the war but the conflict marked the end of Britain's golden cinema age.

Post Second World War to present day

1946 witnessed the greatest number of cinema admissions recorded nationally to date, but audience figures began to fall in the years to follow, albeit slowly at first. By 1953, much of the blame for the increasing decline was attributed to the introduction of television, especially the televising of the Coronation. Later, bingo and ten-pin bowling further contributed to additional falls in cinema attendance. In the post-war economic boom, people's homes became more comfortable and no longer somewhere to escape from to the comfort of a picture palace.

By the early 1960s, many of Camden's popular cinemas had closed. The Court, Gaumont and Gaisford in the Kentish Town area and the Tottenham Court Road Odeon (formerly Paramount) were amongst those lost. In 1961, the former Maida Vale Picture House was said to have become the first commercial bingo hall in the country. The ABC (originally the Forum), Kentish Town also became a bingo hall in 1970. In 1949 Britain boasted 4800 cinemas but, by 1970, this figure had fallen to just over 1500! During the early 1970s, redevelopment schemes in Camden caused the demolition of yet more early cinemas, including the (in)famous Tolmer cinema and three pre-World War One cinemas in Tottenham Court Road.

Although Camden's cinema scene was in decline during the 1970s, not all was lost. A number of newly created or converted cinema buildings appeared. The former Saville Theatre in Shaftesbury Avenue was converted and opened as the ABC in 1970. Later, the independent Bloomsbury cinema and Belsize Park's Screen on the Hill opened in 1972 and 1977, respectively. Camden Town's Plaza was refurbished in 1977 and established itself as one of London's premier art-house cinemas. The 1980s witnessed an upturn in cinema interest and, as a result, Camden saw two more new cinemas open - the Classic, Tottenham Court Road in 1981 and the Curzon Phoenix, off Charing Cross Road in 1987 - but these have proved to be the last to date. Although this revival of interest continued into the 1990s, by 1994 Camden had lost three of its prime cinemas: the Scala at King's Cross and Camden Town's Parkway and Plaza cinemas. For the first time since 1908 Camden Town was without a picture house! There are current proposals to reopen the former Parkway cinema as a multi-screen during 1997, as well as the planned building of a Warner Brothers complex in Finchley Road scheduled to open in 1998.

At present, Camden plays host to eight cinemas. The variety offered in these picture houses caters for many cinematic tastes. Specialist, foreign and independently produced films can be seen at the Everyman, Curzon Phoenix, Renoir and Screen on the Hill cinemas, each possessing a high reputation for quality and unique programming. Meanwhile, mainstream features are supplied by Swiss Cottage's Odeon as well as the ABC cinemas on Shaftesbury Avenue, Tottenham Court Road and Pond Street. The last, much altered over the years, has been a cinema since 1913 when it started life as the Hampstead Picture Playhouse and is currently Camden's longest surviving cinema. Little physically remains of the borough's other former picture palaces, many of which have been demolished or altered beyond recognition, but many will, I hope, be fondly recalled when the following pages are read.

Currency conversion table for ticket prices

Currency pre-1971	Modern decimal currency
1d.(old penny)	.5p (New pence)
2d.	1p
3d	1p
4d	1.5p
5d.	2p
6d.	2.5p
1s.(shilling)	5p
1s 6d.	7.5p
2s.	10p
2s 6d.	12.5p
3s.	15p
3s 6d.	17.5p
4s.	20p
5s.	25p

Taken in 1996, the building pictured in the centre was home to Camden's first permanent cinema, known as the Dara and later the Fan.

Camden's cinemas: an individual history

Camden's cinemas are listed chronologically on the basis of the date on which each building opened as a picture house. The first known name of the cinema is listed first, followed by any later name(s). For easy reference, each cinema has been allocated a serial number.

I Early cinemas

Dara
Fan

1

16-18 Delancey Street, NW1
1908 - 1917

Located in a former Victorian public hall, the Dara first began to show moving pictures around 1908. The building was no stranger to the latest "thing". In 1903 it had been converted for roller skating as the nation took to the pastime in a big way. However, unlike cinema, the roller-skating craze was short-lived.

The Dara was typical of many early cinema conversions, plain in structure with a small

FAN CINEMA

Delancey Street, Camden Town.

THE AFTERNOON THEATRE

WILL YOU TAKE TEA WITH US?

Between 4 and 5 o'clock,

Continuous Performance from 2 to 11 o'clock daily,
Sundays 6 to 11 o'clock.

Afternoon Tea? The Fan (St Pancras Gazette, 29 August 1913).

auditorium. By October 1911, it had been renamed the Fan and was being run independently by the Fan Cinematograph Company. The *St Pancras Gazette* for 19 September 1913 advertised the Fan as Camden Town's "Select Family Picture House". The proprietor was H M Kettlewell. Capacity was estimated at 400-500 seats. As a later inducement to family audiences, the management offered free teas and ice cream to all women and children attending afternoon presentations. Performances were screened from 2pm to 11pm daily and 6pm to 11pm on Sundays. Admission prices varied, with adults paying 1s, 6d and 3d and children 6d, 3d and 2d. In addition, the auditorium boasted a sliding roof.

The cinema also displayed a philanthropic nature. Local newspaper reports show how the Fan regularly gave free performances to nearby institutions. For example, December 1913 saw the building play host to children from the St Pancras Female Orphanage, Hampstead Road, who were treated to "tea and pictures". In 1917, still under the ownership of the Fan Cinematograph Theatre Company, the Fan was refused an operating licence having failed to meet licensing requirements and, as a result, closed. The building never opened again as a cinema. In August 1919, it became a billiard hall, with the sliding roof replaced by glass skylights. Later, it converted to bingo. Today, the former cinema is once again a snooker and billiard hall, being home to the Camden Snooker Club.

Theatre de Luxe

211, High St., Camden Town
Manager - S. BLACKMOORE   'Phone 43 North

'Should a Woman Tell'

An Extremely Stirring Drama in Three Parts, presenting N. A. TZERNOWA.

Showing Exclusively to Camden and Kentish Towns.

THREE DAYS ONLY.
Monday, Feb. 23, to Wednesday, Feb. 25

2 TILL 11 P.M.

Don't Fail to See this Great Picture.

PRICES AS USUAL.

The Theatre Deluxe. It became the Plaza in 1938. Advertisement (St Pancras Gazette, 20 February 1914)

The Plaza, Camden Town in 1982.

Electric Theatre
Theatre Deluxe
Britannia Picture Palace
Plaza

2

211 Camden High Street, NW1
1909 - 29 September 1994

Converted from a bakery, the Electric Theatre opened in 1909. It was operated by Electric Theatres Ltd which ran several other cinemas in London, including the Electric Theatres in Islington and Tufnell Park. By 1914, with a capacity of about 600, the cinema had become the Theatre Deluxe, possibly renamed after the company's Theatre Deluxe cinema in the Strand which had closed that February. In 1919 it became the Britannia Picture Palace, with a seating capacity of 731.

By 1920, the Britannia was changing its programmes three times weekly. In 1934 the company installed a Western Electric Sound System. A little later the same year, the General Cinema Theatre Company acquired the building and in 1937 refurbished the cinema's entrance foyer in a mock Tudor style designed by Cecil Massey. In 1938 it became the Plaza cinema and was again taken over, this time by Town Theatres Ltd, which had also acquired the Gaisford cinema (10) in nearby Kentish Town. Admission prices now ranged from 9d to 2s 5d. However, the company's control of the Plaza was short-lived; in 1942 it became part of the Odeon and later Rank chain. In the years to follow the Plaza gained a seedy reputation and became progressively run-down.

It was not until the 1970s that its shabby reputation was laid to rest. On 9 June 1977, the Plaza reopened as a specialist independent cinema. Its new proprietor was the Artificial Eye company run by Andy and Pam Engel. With a reduced seating of 340, allowing for greater comfort, the first film to be screened at the new Plaza was *Une Partie de Plaisir*. During the 1980s and early 1990s,

the cinema established itself as one of London's premier art film theatres, showing foreign features, independent premieres and the occasional mainstream blockbuster.

Despite its popularity and success, the Plaza was forced to close on 29 September 1994, only a year after two other Camden cinemas, the Parkway (42) in Camden Town and the King's Cross Scala (31), had closed. Earlier that year, the cinema's landlords failed to obtain permission to develop the Plaza site and surrounding area, which also housed the Parkway cinema. Although it won reprieve from closure for another year, the cinema's rent was tripled when its lease was up for renewal. Consequently, payments could not realistically be met and the building was repossessed. The last film to feature at the Plaza was a re-run of the classic *Peeping Tom*. These series of events marked a sad end for what had been one of London's longest surviving picture houses.

To date, the building remains dark. Whilst work is due to start on the conversion of its near neighbour, the Parkway, into a multi-screen Odeon, the Plaza's future remains unresolved.

Kilburn Picture Palace and Theatre of Varieties
Kilburn Picture Palace

③

254-256 Belsize Road, NW6
2 August 1909 - 1941

Constructed in 1888, Hampstead's first building devoted to the presentation of cinematographic film began life as the privately owned Kilburn Town Hall (a local community building not a civic building) before becoming the Kilburn Theatre Royal. It opened as a cinematograph theatre on 2 August 1909, renamed the Kilburn Picture Palace and Theatre of Varieties. Despite its change of use and name, the building was still licensed as the Kilburn Town Hall! Operated by Kilburn Picture Palace Ltd, audiences continued to enjoy live variety acts in support of the main feature film attraction. The theatre's seating capacity was 514. The building's entrance vestibule and auditorium were altered, with the addition of decorative plaster pediments, during the summer of 1910. By 1915 the cinema was known just as the Kilburn Picture Palace and a year later the cinema was correctly licensed

as such under the management, and later proprietorship, of Joseph Clavering. In 1916 further alterations were made to the cinema's auditorium and stage. The Palace was later enlarged to seat 1775.

After the First World War the Palace enjoyed a twice weekly change in programme, with admission prices ranging from 5d to 2s 6d. During the 1920s, the cinema came under the management of Charles Gulliver, who was also managing director of the nearby Kilburn Empire Music Hall (34), itself licensed as a cinema in 1927. In 1928 the Picture Palace had been taken over by United Picture Theatre Ltd (UPT). In July 1930 it was taken over by Gaumont British Pictures while still part of the UPT circuit. During the 1930s, after talkies had been introduced, a British Acoustic Sound System was installed. The Palace finally closed as a cinema late in 1940 and by the end of the Second World War the building was derelict.

In September 1946 the Bloom Brothers, local electrical contractors, leased the building from Gaumont/UPT Ltd hoping to renovate and reopen the cinema, but their plans were never realised. The building later opened as a function hall and rooms. By

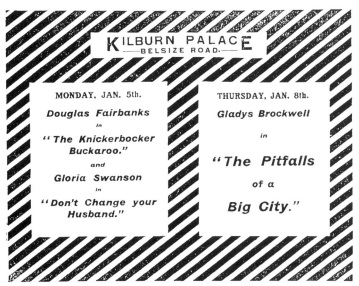

KILBURN PALACE
—— BELSIZE ROAD. ——

MONDAY, JAN. 5th.

Douglas Fairbanks

in

" The Knickerbocker Buckaroo."

and

Gloria Swanson

in

" Don't Change your Husband."

THURSDAY, JAN. 8th.

Gladys Brockwell

in

" The Pitfalls

of a

Big City."

(left) Once home to the Kilburn Picture Palace, the building now houses Decca Recording Ltd.

"No Frills" advertisement for the Kilburn Picture Palace (Kilburn Times, 2 January 1920).

*Euston Cinema
(far left of picture), 1937.*

1953 it had became Shannons Night Club, after which it was used as a warehouse. Currently, the building forms part of the site now occupied by Decca Recording Ltd.

Euston Cinema ④

81 Euston Road, NW1
October 1909 - 1940

Great Northern House on the south side of Euston Road now occupies this site. The Euston was already in operation by October 1909 with 680 seats, under the proprietorship of E M Barker and his Picture Palace Company. Also unofficially known as the Euston Picture Palace, the cinema survived the First World War and, in 1918, was presenting continuous daily performances for 3d to 1s. Still under the control of E Barker, the Euston was managed for a long spell by J Rosenthal. Mr Barker died in June 1926 and his wife took over.

In 1935, under the proprietorship of Euston Cinema Ltd, its capacity was increased to 1154. At this time the Euston's main feature often ran for 6 days with one change on Sundays for a single presentation. The cinema closed around 1940, never to re-open. During World War Two, its interior was reportedly used to house an emergency water tank.

Eldorado Cinematograph Theatre ⑤
Hampstead Picture Palace

64 Heath Street, NW3
1909/1910 - 1916

"A crooked little cinema by the side of Cornick's Yard in Heath Street".

This was how a local resident recalled a visit to this cinema, once situated in the heart of Hampstead village. Sharing its

Free afternoon tea at the Hampstead Picture Palace aka the Electric Theatre (Hampstead and Highgate Express, 18 October 1913).

address with the Hampstead Gymnasium, and located between Streatley Place and Cornick's Yard, 64 Heath Street was converted into a cinema and let to the New Eldorado Cinematograph Theatre Company Ltd. Opening to the public sometime between October 1909 and April 1910, this 200 seat cinema was, not surprisingly, named the Eldorado. However, during July 1910, it was found that the Eldorado was operating unlicensed and was duly prosecuted and fined. The extent of the fine is not known, but the penalty for being unlicensed ranged from 5s to £35. The cinema obviously learned its lesson, as by September the Eldorado was duly licensed.

In 1913 the Eldorado became the Hampstead Picture Palace. Occasionally, it was also known simply as the Electric Theatre, Hampstead. Once again, though, the cinema had licensing problems. In 1915, the mode of operation of the building had to be altered before a new licence could be granted. As before, conditions were soon complied with and on 19 October 1915 the cinema received a new licence, the use of which was but short-lived. By the end of 1916, the Hampstead Picture Palace closed and the following year the building became the Tube Tea Rooms. The site today continues to satisfy appetites and is now a restaurant and cocktail bar.

Gaiety Sphere News Theatre ⑥

28 Tottenham Court Road, W1
4 December 1909 - September 1940

Designed by architect H M Theobald and opened on 4 December 1909, the Gaiety cinema was the first to open in Tottenham Court Road. The Gaiety's 240 seats were all priced at 6d, the first row of seats being 50 ft from the screen. At the outbreak of the First World War, its proprietors were Gaiety Picture Palaces Ltd.

After the war the cinema passed through several private hands. Despite the advent of talking pictures in the late 1920s, it continued to screen silent films, reputedly the last cinema in London to do so. In 1931, its capacity was even extended by a further 94 seats. Cheap seats were still priced at 5d, and only 1s 10d at the top of the range.

By 1933, the Gaiety had closed and the building was redeveloped as a news theatre, a new form of cinema then gaining in popularity. One of the leading architects in the news theatre design was Alistair MacDonald, son of the Labour Prime Minister, who was given the job of converting the Gaiety. Seating was slightly reduced to 238 with seats arranged in short rows of four either side of a central aisle. A Philips Sound System was also installed in the 80ft long auditorium. Reopening on 20 February 1933 as the Sphere News Theatre, the cinema was now under the control of London News Theatres Ltd. Admission prices were still inexpensive at 1s and 7d, with audiences enjoying an hour's varied entertainment. Alistair MacDonald went on later the same year to convert Hampstead's Everyman Theatre(38) to cinema.

The Sphere enjoyed life as a news theatre throughout the 1930s, but closed in September 1940 because of bomb damage and never reopened. Forty years later the site of the Sphere was redeveloped, part of the new development incorporating the Classic cinema(50) which opened in 1981.

by American-born George Washington Grant, operated the 600 seat Kilburn Biograph from 1910 until it closed in 1917. Its licence had expired and application for renewal was not made. A year earlier at the height of the war the Biograph was granted permission to screen charity films on Sundays. All proceeds went to All Saints' Hospital, Vauxhall Bridge Road.

Little is known about the Biograph but its extreme closeness to the 2028 seat Grange Cinema (30), opened in 1914, probably sealed the earlier cinema's fate. It was the third of Hampstead's early picture houses to close during World War One. The former

Biograph Theatre   ⓻
236 Kilburn High Road, NW6
1910 - 1917

Converted from former retail and trade premises, this Kilburn cinematograph theatre was established by Biograph Theatres Ltd, which had earlier opened two other cinemas in London, namely the Parkhurst Cinema Theatre, Holloway, in 1908 and the Electric Theatre in Wilton Road, Victoria, in 1909. The company, run

Biograph building can be seen between the Pizza Hut Restaurant at 238 Kilburn High Road and the Ritz Record Company, Grangeway.

(above) This 1996 view (building to left) was once home to the Biograph Theatre, Kilburn.

(right) Seen here in 1909, the premises to let (adjacent to the florist) became the Gale Cinematograph Hall, Euston Road.

Gale Cinematograph Hall   ⑧
124 Euston Road, NW1
1910 - 1914

This short-lived picture house was situated adjacent to the Rising Sun Public House (now the Friar and Firkin) in Euston Road. Converted from an address previously used by the Euston Motor Company, the building began life as a cinematograph hall around 1910 and was operated by Gale and Company (later Gale and Repard) of 90 Charing Cross Road.

This was another of Camden's early cinemas to close during the First World War. After the war the premises became home to the Association of National People's Palaces. The building is one of the few to survive the heavy 1960s redevelopment of Euston Road, and is in business today as home to both the Chinese Medical Academy and Chinese Travel and Information Centre.

```
COURT                 MALDEN    ROAD,
                      KENTISH   TOWN.
                        GULLIVER 2461

            Sunday, September 19
   Al Jolson, Sybil Jason  THE  SINGING  KID     Ⓤ
   William Gargan, Florence Rice   BLACKMAILER   Ⓐ

   Monday, September 20        For Three Days
   BINKIE STUART          KATHLEEN O'REGAN
   ROSE     OF     TRALEE                        Ⓤ
   George O'Brien
   Irene Ware      O'MALLEY OF THE MOUNTED       Ⓤ

   Thursday, September 23       For Three Days
   JACK  HULBERT          CICELY COURTNEIDGE
   TAKE     MY     TIP                           Ⓤ
   Harry Carey
   Betty Mack      THE LAST OF THE CLINTONS      Ⓤ
```

Irish themed double-bill at the Court (St Pancras Chronicle, 17 September 1937).

Gem Picture Hall
Doric Picture Theatre
Malden Picture Hall
Court
160A Malden Road, NW5
1910 - 19 April 1958

This cinema was possibly Kentish Town's earliest picture house. The Gem Picture Hall, seating a modest 461, opened around 1910 on the corner of Malden Road and Wellesby Place. It was initially under the proprietorship of Albert Letta. In 1919, it had become known as the Doric Picture Theatre. During the early 1920s, the cinema enjoyed two programme changes weekly, with admission priced between 9d and 1s 3d.

The Doric enjoyed only a brief spell under this name, in 1922 it became the Malden Picture House. However, under the new ownership of George Holland, this name was even shorter lived. By the end of the same year the cinema had been renamed the Court. This proved to be its last reincarnation. Long memories recall that the building had a tin roof which played havoc with audience concentration on a wet night, as well as a wooden floor, similarly distracting if hobnail boots were worn! After refurbishment in July 1930, the auditorium featured a proscenium 15 ft wide. It was later installed with an RCA Sound System. Ownership had changed to Percy Holland and ticket prices had actually been reduced, the highest admission being now only 1s.

During the 1930s there was great competition from the newly opened Forum (40) and Odeon(39) super-cinemas in Kentish Town and nearby Haverstock Hill respectively, as well as continuing competition from the area's already established Palace (28) and Gaisford(10) cinemas in Kentish Town Road. However, the Court struggled on, relying heavily on local patronage. Seat prices were very low and the films were usually second-run features. The Court survived the Second World War and continued to provide entertainment for the local population, but by this time the building was extremely tatty.

Despite being run down the cinema played an important social role locally. The following is an account of visits to the Court during the 1940s and 1950s by local resident, and then young filmgoer, Des Whyman:

"Admission price in my time was 1s adult and 6d children. Our family lived down the road in St Silas Street (then Preston Street), six of us in two squalid rooms! As a result, the Court was of major importance in our lives, affording a few hours in the dream world of Hollywood before returning to the poverty and privations of ours. If my memory is correct, at that time the Court was managed by two brothers who, without fail, wore bow tie and evening dress each night, and welcomed you by name. The smart dress was a contradiction in terms considering the

state of the building, very shabby! During each evening at the Court, the usherettes came down the auditorium's two aisles and sprayed pesticide to kill fleas, flies and bugs. To my knowledge it never screened new releases, all the films seemed at least two years old. There was no Saturday morning films unlike the Gaumont, Kentish Town Road (28) either".

But even the neatly dressed staff could not stave off the inevitable. After the screening of its final feature films, *The Silent Enemy* with Laurence Harvey and *The Lawless Eighties* starring John Smith, the cinema closed on 19 April 1958. The building was later demolished to make way for a petrol station which still operates on the site, carrying the memory of the former cinema in its name, this being the Court Service Station.

Kentish Town Cinema Gaisford

1a Gaisford Street, NW5
1910 - 25 June 1960

The Kentish Town Cinema, later became the Gaisford. Advertisement (St Pancras Gazette, 7 September 1917).

The Kentish Town Cinema, situated on the corner of Gaisford Street and Kentish Town Road, was in operation by October

 KENTISH TOWN CINEMA

GAISFORD STREET, N.W. 5.

Manager   Martin Palmer   Telephone : North 2937.

Mon., Tues , & Wed , Sept. 10, 11 & 12 -- | Thurs , Fri , & Sat., Sept. 13, 14, & 15 —
ANNIE LAURIE, | JOHN DREW, DETECTIVE,
In 4 Parts. | In 3 Parts.

THE PURPLE DOMINO (12th Episode) on Thursday. Friday, Saturday, and Sunday.

"AMERICA AWAKES," coming shortly.

Entire Change of Pictures three times weekly, Mon , Thurs , & Sun.

Daily continuous performance, 2 30 till 11 p m.
Sundays (in aid of Local Charities), 6 till 10.30.

Prices, including Government War Tax : 2½d. (Children), 4d., 7d., 1/2 ; but Children's Special PENNY Matinee (unaltered) Saturdays, 1.30.

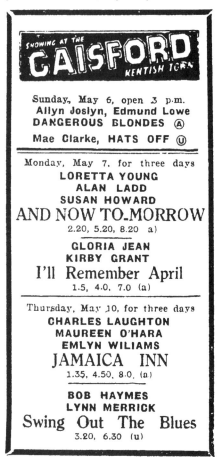

1910. The cinema was initially operated by Kentish Town Cinema Ltd. In later years, it became the Gaisford, and seated 502. Although not as grand as the Palace (28), which opened nearby in 1913, the Kentish Town Cinema was popular with locals.

In 1919 the cinema was taken over by London Cinemas Ltd, which showed second-run features at much cheaper rates than local competitors. By 1928, the cinema offered both pictures and variety on a cramped stage only 6ft in depth! The name was changed in 1933 to the Gaisford. Under the proprietorship of General Cinemas Ltd,

a British Thomson-Houston Sound System was fitted, with ticket prices ranging from 6d to 3s. In 1938 the Gaisford was acquired by Town Theatres Ltd, which had also taken over the Plaza cinema (2) in Camden Town, but by 1942 the cinema had become part of the Odeon chain.

The husband and wife team William and Dorothy Jones managed the cinema from 1945 until the last performance on 25 April 1960, *Code of Silence* and *Lust to Kill*. The cinema was later demolished. Today, Northumberland House, a residential block, occupies the site.

Grand Central Bijou Cineclub 24
24 Tottenham Court Road, W1
12 February 1910 - 1931
11 September 1969 - 24 December 1976

L ocated only two doors from the Gaiety (6), the Grand Central opened on 12 February 1912 converted from a former china-ware shop. Sister cinema to the Majestic and Carlton (23;27), also on Tottenham Court Road, and under the proprietorship of Grand Central Ltd, the Grand was designed by Keenes Purchase. It had 395 seats, only 41 of them with armrests! There was a sliding roof for use during hot summers. In view of the strong competition, many attempts were made to entice audiences in. The Grand offered tea and cake to those visiting between 4pm and 6pm and, later, introduced a three-piece orchestra.

In 1928, following a change in ownership, the cinema was renamed the Bijou, but this lasted only until around 1931 when it closed. For the next four decades or so the site reverted to retail use. However, on 11 September 1969 Cineclub 24 opened its doors to members. With a seating capacity of 250, and run by the Cinecenta group, the building enjoyed a further 7 years of business, finally closing on Christmas Eve 1976. It was demolished during the late 1970s as part of a redevelopment scheme that also claimed the former Carlton, Majestic and Gaiety cinemas, but part of the new development incorporated a new cinema, the Classic (50), which opened in 1981.

Kilburn Electric Palace Cosy Corner Cinema
10 Kilburn High Road, NW6
21 April 1910 - 1916

The Kilburn Picture Palace opened on Thursday 21 April 1910. At the grand opening ceremony Princess Marie Louise of Bourbon (Duchess of Seville) declared; "Till lately, seeing the world was only possible to the wealthy but owing to the marvellous invention, the most beautiful scenery could be admired for a few pence, while safe from the risks of travelling". Today, the Princess's simple yet accurate observation is taken wholly for granted. The Princess was received by Captain A E Raikes, chairman of the Kilburn Electric Palace Company. The cinema's pianist, Miss Janotha, played a Humouresque Sevigliana composed by herself in honour of the Princess. Following the official opening ceremony, a special charity film performance was given with all proceeds going to St Mary's Hospital.

By 1914 the Kilburn Electric Palace had been renamed the Cosy Corner Cinema. But the Cosy closed in 1916. By this time Kilburn was flourishing as an entertainment area, but this made competition fierce and may have contributed to the cinema's demise. In 1917 Cosy Corner's site became the Kilburn Garage. The building, along with the nearby Kilburn Empire (34), was later demolished to make way for a new hotel, the Regents Plaza which opened in 1996.

Holborn Cinema Embassy
210-211 High Holborn, WC1
15 October 1910 - 1925

The Holborn Cinema opened at 210-211 High Holborn on 15 October 1910. Designed by F W Foster for Holborn Cinemas Ltd, the building seated 472, with a tea lounge on the first floor. After World War One the cinema was enjoying three programme changes weekly, admission being from 9d to 3s 6d. The British-Franco Sign Company took over the picture house in 1920. In September 1923, after a number of alterations by architect Frank Verity, it became the Embassy. At this time a live variety show was added to support the main feature film, but by 1925 the cinema had closed and the premises were taken over by a company making metal casements. The address is now home to a branch of Midland Bank and adjoining offices.

Corner Theatre Grafton Cinematograph Theatre
134a Tottenham Court Road, W1
16 November 1910 - 1929

A McDonald's restaurant now occupies the site of this former basement cinema. Opened on 16 November 1910, with 280 seats and room for 50 standing, the Corner Theatre adopted its second name in 1911. During the 1920s, admission was 5d to 1s 3d and there were three programme changes a week. By 1929 the cinema had closed. From 1930 to 1940 the building functioned as the Grafton Theatre, with live shows. After World War Two, the BBC used it as a studio for over 20 years.

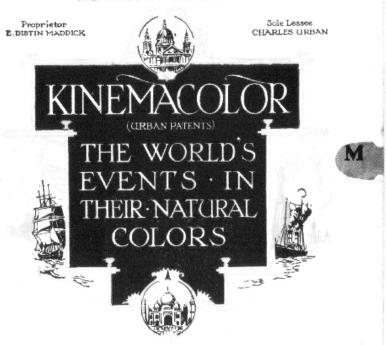

SCALA THEATRE
· CHARLOTTE · STREET · W ·

Proprietor
E. DISTIN MADDICK

Sole Lessee
CHARLES URBAN

KINEMACOLOR
(URBAN PATENTS)

THE WORLD'S EVENTS · IN THEIR·NATURAL COLORS

TWICE DAILY · · 2.30 and 8.

(left) Auditorium of the Scala Theatre when in use as a cinema in 1912. (above) "Kinemacolor" at the Scala, 1912.

Scala Theatre ⑮

25 Tottenham Street, W1
1911 - 1913

This famous theatre became a full-time cinema between 1911 and 1913, when the American Charles Urban presented his very popular Kinemacolor shows. In 1913 these transferred to another Camden cinema, the Maida Vale Picture Palace (25).

After its return to live theatre, the Scala periodically presented film premieres. In September 1915, D W Griffith's *Birth of a Nation* received its first British showing at the Scala. Russian film seasons were often held during the 1950s. The Scala Theatre was demolished in 1970 and replaced with a residential/office block. In 1976, the Other Cinema Club (48) began operating in a basement on the site, becoming the Scala Cinema Club(48) which relocated to King's Cross in 1981. The site is now occupied by Channel One, a cable television company. The theatre is still remembered at 21 Tottenham Street where Scala House, an apartment block, can be found.

"The World Through The Camera" at the Alhambra (St Pancras Gazette, 28 July 1911).

Electric Alhambra ⑯

303-305 Kentish Town Road, NW5
20 February 1911 - c.1918

On 20 February 1911 the Mayor of St Pancras, Councillor F W Avant, opened the Electric Alhambra Cinematograph Theatre. All proceeds of the first night were donated to St Pancras Charities, the cinema's managing director, Philip Beck, adding a personal 5 guineas to the collection. The Alhambra's architectural and interior designs were co-ordinated by M Marsland. Part of the design was a "well appointed" tea room, with a separate entrance in adjacent Holmes Road accessible to ladies and children if they wished, without going into the theatre! The 500-seat auditorium had stalls and balcony areas, the latter costing 1s for a "comfort-able" seat. Other charges were 3d, 6d and 9d.

The Alhambra's programmes included the latest features and a series of scientific films or, as one local newspaper advert suggested, audiences could see the "world through the camera". Indeed, customers were told at the opening that films presented would be interesting, elevating and instructive as well as amusing!

Despite an auspicious opening and presentation of elevating films, the Electric Alhambra did not last long. It closed during 1918, having failed to renew its licence. Shortly after closure the former cinema

---

ELECTRIC ALHAMBRA,

303 & 305, KENTISH TOWN ROAD, N.W.

Nearly opposite Kentish Town Tube Station.

THE WORLD THROUGH THE CAMERA.

Always Star Programme.   Change Sundays, Mondays, & Thursdays

OPEN ON SUNDAYS.

PRICES OF ADMISSION, 3d., 6d., 9d., and 1s.

---

became a billiards hall. During the 1930s Marks and Spencer established their Kentish Town store on the site and stayed there for the next 50 years. Today, the building is an Iceland Ltd food store.

Frognal Bijou Picture Palace ⑰
Frognal Picture House
Odette's Picture House
Frognal Picture House
Arcadia Picture Palace
Casino Picture Palace
New Frognal Cinema
158 Finchley Road, NW3
13 April 1911 - 1931

"An admirably equipped and prettily decorated little theatre, and a gem of its kind".

This was how the *Hampstead Advertiser* for 20 April 1911 described Finchley Road's new Bijou Picture Palace upon opening. Situated diagonally opposite what is now Finchley Road Underground Station, and converted from former shops, the Frognal Bijou Picture House opened on 13 April 1913.

Designed by a local architect, identity unknown, the Bijou's seating capacity was relatively small at 240 seats, each uphol-stered in blue damask. Its interior decor was white, with shaded blue panels, draperies and pile carpet to match. The Bijou's staff, or "officials", wore uniforms of black and gold with red waistcoats. The cinema's first films were mainly educational travelogues. Management boasted that "nothing but the very best pictures shall be placed before the public ...and [these] will appeal to all classes". Upon opening, the audiences enjoyed *Niagara and other Beauties of the World,* as well as a series of comedy film sketches with Mr Harrington supplying the piano accompaniment. Initially, programmes covered two separate houses, each providing two hours of entertainment. Programmes

changed every Monday and Thursday; admission charges were 1s and 6d with children half price. Patrons could also enjoy light refreshment in the Bijou's tea lounge.

Soon, however, the Bijou incurred the wrath of many local residents by deciding to open on Sundays. The cinema had successfully applied for permission to allow presentation of films on Sundays in accordance with the regulation that halls could be rented on Sundays to educational and charitable institutions, in this case the London Hospital. Nonetheless, this brought a storm of protest from locals. The campaign to have the Bijou close on Sundays being spear-headed by the Rev H Summerhayes, vicar of neighbouring Trinity Church. In the cinema's defence the Bijou Syndicate's secretary, Henry Duke, argued that the

The New Frognal Cinema advertisement (Hampstead Advertiser, 27 December 1928).

building was rented for charitable purposes. Duke was prepared to hold a referendum which would be binding on the syndicate. During this scandal, the *Hampstead and Highgate Express* received a petition containing the names of 153 residents calling for the Bijou to close on Sundays. Nevertheless, in spite of opposition, the cinema managed to renew its Sunday privileges the following July.

By 1915 the Bijou had become the Frognal Picture House, and in 1921 Odette's Picture House, after the dance hall next door. The name alternated between this and the Frognal Picture House twice more. In 1924 the cinema became the Arcadia Picture Palace, with a continuous programme between 3pm and 11pm, and free teas between 3 and 6pm. Briefly as the Casino Picture Palace, the former Bijou was finally known from 1925 as the New Frognal Cinema. It closed around 1931, possibly because the expense of conversion to talkies was too great for such a small picture house. It was later put to retail use. Midland Court, a residential block, now occupies the site.

Coronation Gardens Cinema ⑱
Garden Cinema
Prince of Wales Road, NW5
1 July 1911 - 1913 (Seasonal)

"One of the most startling, novel and original

Coronation Gardens
CINEMA,
PRINCE OF WALES ROAD, KENTISH TOWN
(Nearly opposite the Baths).

LONDON'S LATEST NOVELTY.

ANIMATED PICTURES
In the OPEN AIR.

GRAND OPENING. to-morrow. SATURDAY. at 7 p.m..

And each evening during the season. Gates Open at 6.30.
Ground Open for inspection from 3 to 6 p.m.

Complete Change of Programme Every Monday & Thursday.

POPULAR PRICES, 3d. & 6d.

These Beautiful and Romantic Old-World Gardens will be brilliantly
Illuminated, and the Pictures will be shown Continuously from 7 to 11 p.m.
Under the Management of
MR. ERNEST MANSELL, Proprietor of the popular "King's Service" Pictures.

SPECIAL NOTICE.
Commencing on Sunday, July 9th, and Every Sunday during the Season,
a Special Programme will be presented from 8 to 10. Gates open 7.30.
ADMISSION by "COUPON PROGRAMME" only,
which may be obtained in the Grounds during the week.

J. H. PORTMAN, Secretary,
CORONATION GARDENS CINEMA CO.,
Chief Office:—241, Marylebone Road, W.

innovations connected with the picture world of London has just been introduced..."

So stated the *St Pancras Gazette* (30 June 1911) when this open-air cinema opened. Under the management of Ernest Mansell, who had earlier presented programmes of moving pictures at the Kentish Town Baths opposite, this al fresco enterprise was initiated by Portmans Ltd of Marylebone Road.

The site itself, formerly the grounds of the area's Reform Club, became known, after landscaping, as the Coronation Gardens. The first performance took place on Saturday 1 July 1911 with a variety presentation of pictures. Continuous performances were shown between 7pm and 11pm weekdays and between 8pm and 10pm on Sundays. Admission prices were 3d and 6d. Also advertised as an added feature was the use of pictures filmed using non-flam, a special non-combustible film.

The operation of the cinema was seasonal, with performances taking place only in July and August. 1913 marked the venture's last season and, by this time, it had become simply known as the Gardens Cinema. In this final season it showed a series entitled *Life in the King's Service,* ominous given the date. The gardens later supported the buildings of the Polytechnic/University of North London, which vacated the location in 1995. Currently, the former University site awaits redevelopment.

Court Cinema ⑲
Court Imperial Cinema
Court Playhouse Cinema
Court Picture Palace
268 Tottenham Court Road, W1
October 1911 - March 1928

The foyer of the Dominion Theatre (35) now occupies the site of the former Court Cinema. The Court was later to become one of a number of cinemas run by London

(opposite page) Pictures "al fresco!"
(St Pancras Gazette, 30 June 1911).
(above) The Court Cinema, Tottenham Court
Road, (far right of picture) in 1912.
(left) Typical fare at the Court, Tottenham Court
Road, with free teas and ices, in 1918.

and Provincial Electric Theatres. An early attraction accompanying features at the 240 seat cinema was an Italian Orchestra. On Easter Monday, 1912, the cinema played host to the country's first film trade show. The film *Christopher Columbus* was screened to visiting exhibitors during the event. In 1915 new owners changed the name to the Court Imperial Cinema, which was re-sold in 1917 as the Court Playhouse Cinema to the Kingley Cinema Company. Prices after World War One ranged from 9d to 2s 6d and free teas or ices were served to all patrons between 3pm and 5.30pm.

In May 1924 the cinema, now the Court Picture Palace, came under the management of H Silverman and acquired a reputation for showing sex films. Indeed, as a result of screening a controversial film, the cinema was closed in March 1928. The building was almost certainly due to close in any case, to make way for the Dominion.

Fitzroy Picture Palace Electric Theatre

20

64a (now 69) Charlotte Street, W1
1912 - 1916

Once located opposite the famous Scala Theatre(15) which was also showing films around the same time, the Fitzroy Picture Palace's life was but short-lived. Established around 1912 on the corner of Tottenham Street and Charlotte Street, its seating capacity was small at 173. It was re-named the Electric around 1914/15 whilst under the proprietorship of Messrs Tanner and Goldberg, but in 1916 it joined the many picture houses which closed down, never to reopen, during the First World War. A take-away food shop now stands on the site.

Electric Palladium

21

143 Camden High Street, NW1
January 1912 - 1927

Once situated on a site now occupied by Marks and Spencer retailers, this Camden Town cinema began operating in 1912. Although still under construction in October 1911, a conditional licence was granted to its proprietress Mrs Hannah Abrahams and her architect son C Clarence.

In 1915, and still under the same management, the Palladium was completely redecorated and re-upholstered. Following refurbishment, the *St Pancras Gazette* for 12 February 1915, describing management policy, stated: "The concern is entirely British. No aliens have, are or will be employed" - clearly at the height of First World War anti-German fever. The 600 seat cinema enjoyed three programme changes weekly, with all performances accompanied by the Palladium's "first-class" orchestra. By 1919, under new management, the Palladium was offering two weekly programme changes; admission prices were 5d to 1s 3d.

The cinema continued until 1927, when the building was acquired and rebuilt by Marks and Spencers, who had moved from smaller premises a few doors away at 133 Camden High Street.

Avenue Picture Palace

22

Pratt Street, NW1
April 1912 - c.1915

This short-lived and little-known picture house in Pratt Street was converted from a former Baptist Chapel adjacent to Camden Town's fire station. The Avenue's proprietor was Michael William Shanley. The cinema closed in 1915, another victim of the war period.

However, Mr Shanley went on to greater things. By 1921, he had established Shanley's Animated Pictures at 35 King Henry's Road, Primrose Hill. This company ran a chain of cinemas in the south of England and in Ireland. The Pratt Street building was later demolished and residential flats (124 Pratt Street) now partly occupy the site.

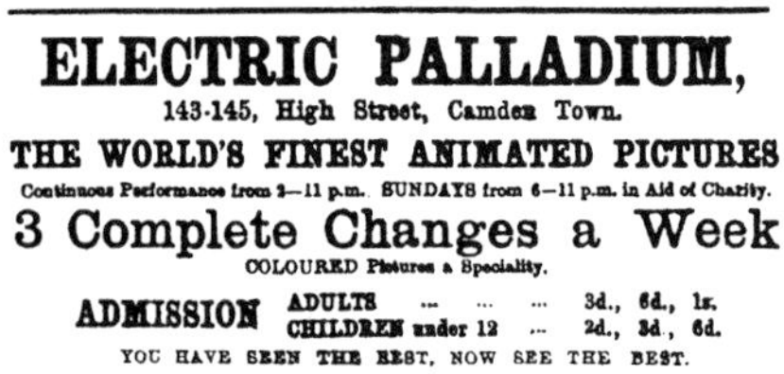

Marks and Spencer now occupy the site of the former Electric Palladium, Camden Town. Early advertisement (St Pancras Gazette, 5 January 1912).

Majestic Picturedrome La Continentale

36 Tottenham Court Road, W1
4 May 1912 - 31 August 1976

As the older sister to the nearby Carlton cinema (27), the Majestic Picturedrome was one of the earliest purpose-built cinemas in the area, its site previously occupied by a coffee house. With proprietor Grand Central Ltd and designs by Peter Dollar, the 640 seat Majestic opened to the public on 4 May 1912. The auditorium featured a dome 60ft in circumference which

(above) Majestic Picturedrome, 1912. Its modest entrance concealed a more "majestic" interior.

(below) The Majestic's splendid auditorium and dome, 1912.

contained twelve panels depicting angels which were lit up during intervals. The auditorium's proscenium was 20ft wide.

Until the 1930s the cinema screened first-run features, but by January 1940, after several changes in ownership, the Majestic had closed, probably because of dwindling audiences, increased competition and the attractions of larger West End theatres. However, the cinema reopened on 25 October 1942. On 24 April 1948, it was renamed La Continentale and showed mainly foreign films. By the 1970s, programming included current mainstream releases and its seating capacity had been reduced to 440.

La Continentale closed on 31 August 1976, the same day as its sister the Berkeley (originally Carlton). The site was later redeveloped as part of a retail and business complex which included a new cinema, the Classic (50), which opened in 1981.

By January 1913, under the ownership of Biocolor Picture Theatre Ltd, the theatre had become a fully-fledged cinema, although film seasons at the theatre were being advertised as early as 1911.

The original seating capacity was 1600 but, including standing room, the live theatre could take an audience of up to 2434. During the 1920s, live acts supported the film presentations. In 1928 Friday nights became "Novelty Night", when up to seven acts could be seen before the main features. In 1933, now being run by Gaumont British Pictures, the Hippodrome was installed with a British Acoustic Sound System. The cinema also began to stage Christmas and New Year performances for local children. On the morning of 6 January 1933, the cinema played host to over 1000 children with a free film performance, together with free bags of fruit and sweets! The event was attended by St Pancras Mayor, Sidney Bolsom. In March, London County Council's Education Department began to hire the Hippodrome for special educational screenings, for example (17 March) *The Life Story of a Swallow-tail Butterfly*, for school children aged 8-11, the cinema's hire charge being £5.

The cinema closed sometime after April 1940. In 1945 the building became home to the BBC's Theatre Orchestra, which stayed for over two decades. After threat of demolition in the 1970s, Camden Council gave permission for the building to reopen as a nightclub. It later became Nero's, a dance club with live music; the Music Machine, a mainly live music venue; and since 1982, the Camden Palace, a popular live music and dance club. It was listed Grade II in 1991.

(opposite page) Camden Hippodrome, 1928. The building survives today as the Camden Palace nightclub.

(above) Interior of the Camden Hippodrome, 1928. The boxes either side of the screen reveal its former theatrical past.

Camden Hippodrome (Picture Theatre) ㉔

1a Camden High Street, NW1
1913 - 1940

Designed by W G R Sprague, this building was originally opened on Boxing Day, 1900 as the Camden Theatre by the actress Ellen Terry. On 6 December 1909 it became the Hippodrome, home to variety.

Maida Vale Picture Palace
Maida Vale Picture House

25

140 Maida Vale, W9
27 January 1913 - 1940

Plans and drawings submitted by architect George Duckworth, seeking permission for the building of this purpose built cinema, were first accepted by the LCC (London County Council) on 17th October 1911 but the plans were never realised. Instead, designs drawn up by Edward A Stone, were later used and, in

a little over twelve months, the Maida Vale Picture Palace opened to the public on 27th January 1913.

The *Hampstead Advertiser* announced that Kinemacolor from the Scala Theatre (15), Tottenham Street had arrived in Maida Vale and could be viewed at the new Maida Vale Picture Palace. Under the control of Maida Vale Picture Palace Ltd, the cinema's opening feature was *Behind the Mask* starring Saharet, the renowned dancer! Programming policy was to show premiere, first run films. Accompanying film presentations was a "magnificent" seven piece orchestra, under

the baton of conductor T M Paiba, and supported by the Palace's Organ.

Hailed in local newspaper advertising as London's most luxurious picture theatre, the *Kilburn Times* for 24th January 1913 described the exterior of the Palace, with it's two main towers and coppered domes, as "dignified and imposing". The entrance vestibule had a marble floor and a grand Georgian mantlepiece with a dog grate, said to give "a touch of homeliness which was usually lacking in a vestibule of this kind"! Total seating was 1,500, with a 500 seat balcony including a number of curtained boxes. The auditorium was raked, with walls panelled with figured oak and fibrous plaster, whilst overlooked by a domed ceiling. The Palace's colour scheme was royal blue and old gold. Its screen measured 20ft x 15ft. Performances at the Picture Palace were continuous between 2.30pm (later 3pm) and 11pm. Programmes changed every Monday and Thursday, with admission prices ranging between 6d, 1s, and 2s, with boxes priced at 10s 6d and 7s 6d. Discount books of tickets could also be purchased. Before a performance patrons could relax in the cinema's lounge or in the tea room which was "daintily" decorated in Adam style. The cinema also boasted a telephone booking facility. By May 1913, the orchestra's leader was Signor T Del Perugia, gold medallist of the Florence Conservatoire of Music. One local newspaper asserted that the orchestra's standards were now "exceptionally high!"

In the summer of 1916, Edison's Kinetophone Talking Pictures were a popular attraction, showing every weekday performance. By 1921 the Palace witnessed a change in operator. Control was now under the auspices of Scala (Maida Vale) Ltd, a subsidiary of Provincial Cinematograph Theatres. Two years later there was a slight change in name, to the Maida Vale Picture House. In 1927, proprietorship was transferred to Associated Provincial Picture Houses, with admission now priced between 8d and 3s. The same year a new Grand Wurlitzer Organ was installed, powerful enough to disturb local residents in Greville Place, three of whom opposed renewal of the Palace's cinematograph licence, arguing that the organ could be plainly heard outside the cinema, causing a "definite, constant and serious nuisance with organ notes escaping freely". Nevertheless, the cinema licence was granted, doubtless to the anxiety of the local residents!

During the 1920s, the cinema also gave seasonal charity performances to local children. At Christmas 1928, for example, children watched Charlie Chaplin and Jackie Coogan films and were entertained afterwards by famous bass singer Senor Enrico Garcia, who later took part in a carol service with the children accompanied by full orchestra and infamous organ! In February 1929 the cinema came under the umbrella of the huge Gaumont British Picture Corporation and showed talkies throughout the 1930s. The Picture House closed in November 1940 and never reopened as a cinema but the following year a restaurant was operating in the building.

In 1949 the former cinema reopened as the Carlton Rooms, a social club and entertainment venue. Live broadcasts by well known dance bands, including that of Victor Sylvester, became a popular feature. In 1961 the Carlton became a Mecca Social Club, reported to be the first commercial bingo hall in the country. Thirty years later, on 5 February 1991, the building was listed Grade II. The Carlton Rooms played host to bingo until early 1996 but now remains dark. Although in need of external decoration, the building's frontage still remains dignified and imposing, allowing on-lookers to visualise how the Maida Vale Picture Palace must have appeared during its glory days.

Maida Vale Picture Palace, 1920. The building still survives in 1997.

Hampstead Picture Playhouse
Hampstead Playhouse
Classic, Hampstead
Cannon, Hampstead
MGM, Hampstead
ABC, Hampstead

Pond Street, NW3
4 August 1913 - present

Hampstead Picture Playhouse. An early advertisement (Hampstead and Highgate Express, 13 September 1913).

Described by the *Daily Chronicle* as being "perhaps the most beautiful [cinematograph theatre] in London", the Hampstead Picture Playhouse officially opened on 4th August 1913, although the cinema was open free to Hampstead residents on the previous Saturday for a sneak preview! Designed by T Millwood Wilson of Staple Inn, Holborn, it was under the proprietorship of F Green and Hampstead Picture Playhouse Ltd.

The building's exterior received a "quiet and dignified treatment of the Renaissance style of architecture, so much in contrast with the usual florid elevations we are accustomed to see in this class of building" (*Hampstead & Highgate Express*, 9 August 1913). The interior too received generous

review. There was a double-doored foyer entrance and the auditorium had a curved ceiling richly ornamented with large modelled plaster bands and ventilation openings. Powerful fans were installed to bring continuous fresh air from the nearby heath! The plaster-work walls were of a "chaste" design and set amongst a backdrop of blue-grey and white, with hangings of deep blue. The Picture Playhouse's 1500 seats were of old gold velvet. Even the cheap seats had arms and, for those who required "the acme of luxury", twin-seat settee lounges were available in the balcony. The building also boasted a dual system of lighting, in case one failed!

The opening feature was *The Spectre of the Sea*, with musical entertainment provided by E J Parker's special orchestra. The management emphasised that no "questionable films will be shown on the premises and horrors are barred. The ordinary legitimate drama, the presentation of healthy adventure, the reproduction of beautiful scenes and the marvellous portrayal of nature's wonders will hold the attention of the audience". Weekday and Saturday performances were continuous from 3pm. There was a telephone booking system. Area stalls were 3d and 6d and balcony stalls 1s, settee lounges were 1s 6d per person, and admission for children was 2d, 4d, 6d or 1s. Therefore, with a modern design, a comfortable and large auditorium, a varied, morally correct programme policy, little local competition and a convenient situation adjacent to the tramway terminus and the area's railway station, the Hampstead Picture Playhouse's success was assured.

Within a short time, guest soloists were invited to play with Mr Parker's orchestra, often with many encores requested following the screening of the main feature. Programming also became more adventurous. In January 1914, the acclaimed but lengthy film *Protea* was screened with eight other attractions and, in consequence, audiences attending the complete programme witnessed nearly two miles of pictures! Later, Kinema Poems were introduced, in which live actors verbally synchronised the on-screen actors' lip movements.

After the First World War, the cinema enjoyed three changes in programme per week. During the 1920s, the Playhouse also became known for its charitable deeds. In May 1926 a free matinee performance was held for over 1000 poor London children during the General Strike. At the other end of the social spectrum, national celebrities attended performances at the Playhouse. Famous star of stage and screen and Hampstead resident Sir Gerald Du Maurier and fellow thespian Gladys Cooper regularly attended matinees in 1927. Additional attractions now included regular free cinema lectures given on Sunday afternoons, for example a film about the slum clearance work of the St Pancras House Improvement Society at Somers Town (2 November 1930).

For several years the Playhouse received LCC permission to present religious charity presentations on Good Fridays. In 1929, *INRI* was screened with choral music accompaniment, all proceeds going to St Dominic's Priory Poor Children's Outing Fund and St Stephen's Church Poor Fund. The following year the cinema's Good Friday film was *Christus*, proceeds again going to these charities. However, the next year permission was refused. Perhaps the addition of a religious service to accompany the featured film was a little too adventurous for the LCC!

On 31 March 1930 the Playhouse screened its first talking picture: *High Treason*, starring James M Thomas. However, silent films were still shown in support and the cinema still retained a full orchestra. For one week in August 1931, the Playhouse was closed for redecoration and installation of the state-of-the-art Western Electric Sound System. During the 1930s, the Playhouse was granted local authority permission to use the building every Christmas to hold parties for local children.

The cinema closed during most of World War Two, reopening in 1946 under the slightly shortened name of the Hampstead Playhouse. During the 1950s, the wide-screen innovation Cinemascope was introduced. On 7 February 1965, the cinema became the Classic, having been taken over by the cinema chain of the same name. During the Hampstead Festival of the Arts in the summer of 1965, the Classic screened a season of opera films. In 1968 the building was modernised. New seating arrangements, with a reduced capacity of 1120, followed the

MGM, Pond Street (began life as the Hampstead Picture Playhouse) in 1996. Now an ABC cinema

Continental pattern of having the best seats in the stalls instead of the circle. A new wide screen was also installed.

On 25 May 1978, the cinema reopened as a triple-screen complex bearing little resemblance to the original Playhouse design. Screen 1 now had only 265 seats, Screen 2 190 and Screen 3 188 seats. In 1984, Screen 3 was renamed the Heath, specialising in art-house movies. However, this foray into the non-mainstream world proved short-lived and the Heath returned to screening first-run major releases. The whole became the Cannon in 1985, under the management of the Cannon cinema group.

During early 1986, a fire badly damaged the cinema but it reopened in July, Screen 1 now seating 476. The cinema now introduced late-night screenings on Saturdays. In 1991, as with others in the Cannon group, following its parent company Pathe's acquisition of the MGM/UA group, the cinema became the MGM. During 1995 the Virgin Company took over the running of the MGM chain but only a year later the company sold part of its interest in the chain to a newly resurrected ABC group. Not surprisingly the Pond Street cinema is now known as the ABC, Hampstead.

Today, the ABC's programme of mainstream first-run films complements the specialist art-house and repertory programming of its nearest neighbours, the Screen on the Hill (49) and the Everyman Cinema (38). Sadly, nothing remains of its original facade or interior decor but the building has remained

An advertisement for the Carlton, Tottenham Court Road and its sister cinema (St Pancras Chronicle, 11 May 1945).

faithful to moving pictures for over 80 years and currently holds the record for being Camden's longest surviving cinema.

Carlton Berkeley ㉗
30 Tottenham Court Road, W1
October 1913 - 31 August 1976

The Carlton opened in October 1913 and was the younger sister of the Majestic Picturedrome (23) at 36 Tottenham Court Road. The two were run by Grand Central until 1928. The plans a year later to demolish the Carlton and the Grand Central cinema (11) at 24 Tottenham Court Road to make way for a super-cinema on the site were never realised. Following a succession of proprietors during the 1930s, the Carlton

CARLTON
Tottenham Court Road, W.1
Phone Museum 8150

FOR THREE WEEKS

ADULTS ONLY

MARCELLE CHANTAL
JEAN YONNEL

AMOK

(French Dialogue, English Sub-titles)

Children under 16 are Not permitted to see this film

ALSO

DEANNA DURBIN

HIS BUTLER'S SISTER Ⓤ

THE WORLD'S NEWS IN PICTURES

Continuous from 1 o'clock

MAJESTIC
Tottenham Court Road, W.1
Phone Museum 4790

Thursday, May 3, for three days
**PRESTON FOSTER
LLOYD NOLAN**

Guadalcanal Diary Ⓐ

ALSO
**LINDA DARNELL
EDGAR BUCHANAN**

City Without Men Ⓐ

Sunday, May 6, for four days
**DON AMECHE
FRANCES DEE**

HAPPY LAND Ⓤ

ALSO
**GORDON HARKER
ELIZABETH ALLEN**

SALOON · BAR Ⓐ

Sunday Open 3 p.m.

closed between 1939 and 1943 due to a drop in business.

In April 1948 the Carlton was refurbished and became the Berkeley, now specialising in premieres of foreign films. The building underwent further modernisation in 1959 and 1969, and on 3 May 1973 a second but smaller 183-seat auditorium was established, the Berkeley 2. Together with the Majestic, by this time known as La Continentale, the Berkeley finally closed on 31 August 1976. The last films to be shown were *Sin of Father Mouret* and *Switchboard Operator* at the Berkeley, whilst *Lennie* and *The Decameron* saw out Berkeley 2. Its closure made way for a new building complex. From this emerged the present ABC (originally Classic) cinema(50), Tottenham Court Road, which opened on 30 July 1981.

PALACE CINEMA

KENTISH TOWN ROAD, Prince corner of Road, N.W

'Phone Hampstead 1493

One minute from South Kentish Town Station (Tube) and three minutes' from Kentish Town Station (Midland and Tube). Busses and trams pass the door.

THE GRAND OPENING

of this magnificent Theatre, accommodating 1,000 people, will take place on

Monday, December 8th, at 7.30 p.m. by

HIS WORSHIP THE MAYOR, Coun. T. A. Collins, J.P.

On this occasion and during the Week will be shown the

HOUSE OF TEMPERLEY

The Finest British Picture ever produced, showing a Marvellous Representation of a

PRIZE FIGHT in good Old English Style.

Also a Stupendous Programme of the Finest Pictures.

THE MAGNIFICENT RUSSIAN ORCHESTRA will perform both at Afternoon and Evening Performances.

Continuous Performance 2.30 to 11 p.m.   Sundays commence at 6 o'clock.

Prices of admission :

STALLS 3d. and 6d.   GRAND CIRCLE 9d. and 1s.   Children Half-Price.

*Opening advertisement for the Palace
(St Pancras Gazette, 5 December 1913).*

Palace
Gaumont, Kentish Town   (28)
197 Kentish Town Road, NW5
8 December 1913 - 4 April 1959

Early architectural plans show that the cinema was to be named the Criterion. However, initially operated by Palatial Cinemas Ltd and later by Provincial Cinematograph Theatres, the building first opened as the Palace Cinema in 1913. Designed by a young John Stanley Beard, the cinema boasted 1052 seats. Officiating at its grand opening was the Mayor of St Pancras, T A Collins. Its premiere feature was Sir Arthur Conan Doyle's *The House of Temperley*, then only the 10th British full-length feature film. This and all subsequent performances were accompanied by a Russian Orchestra. Admission prices were stalls 3d and 6d, Grand Circle 9d and 1s and children half price.

During the First World War the Palace also staged regular recruiting drives, appealing for young men to "perform their duty". Patriotic films were shown, often supported with a speech from an officer or recruiting

sergeant. If convinced, men could sign up for active service afterwards in the cinema. For the next 20 years, the Palace was to be the leading player in the Kentish Town cinema scene, the position being reaffirmed with the coming of talkies. Live variety acts had by then been added to its Friday night programme. In February 1929 Gaumont British Pictures took over Provincial Cinematograph Theatres and with it the Palace.

"The Palace is to be congratulated on possessing such an up-to-date apparatus, and the management on their enterprising policy...the privilege of seeing and hearing such a picture would cost a guinea in New York, in the West End 5s 9d but here the price was as low as 6d !" Thus spoke St Pancras Mayor, H E Capes, at a ceremony marking the installation for talkies of the cinema's new Western Electric Sound System on 5 May 1930. Talkies had actually arrived at the Palace by October 1929, *The Four Devils* starring Janet Gaynor being one of the first to be featured. The first talking picture to be screened that evening using the new system was Erich von Stroheim's *The Great Gabbo*.

By 1948, the Palace had become the Gaumont. It closed 11 years later on 4 April 1959, its last films being *The Black Orchid* starring Sophia Loren and an early Charles Bronson feature entitled *When Hell Broke Loose*. Part of the building was later demolished to make way for a warehouse. The Bloomsbury and Hampstead Community Health Councils currently occupy the cinema's former address. Around the corner in Prince of Wales Road part of the exterior of the former Palace, now home to the Camden Law Centre, can still be seen.

(right) Palace, Kentish Town in 1913. It later became the Gaumont.

(below) The Palace's decorative interior, 1913.

Lismore ㉙

37-39 Lismore Road, NW5
April 1914 - 1917

A largely forgotten picture palace in Camden's Gospel Oak area, the Lismore was a venture lasting only a few years. The picture house was created by converting two dining rooms that had previously existed on the site, one being a fried-fish shop under the management of the marvellously named Mrs Phoebe Gue!

Under the ownership of James Kerrison and to the designs of Albert Smith, the Lismore opened sometime after April 1914. Seating about 500 on a single raked floor, the cinema also featured an orchestra. However, by 1917 the Lismore's licence had expired and was not renewed. The cinema became a temperance billiard hall. There is nothing left of the building after the Lismore Road redevelopment of the late 1960s. The forecourt of the housing block Ludham (near Mansfield Road) now covers the site of Gospel Oak's only cinema.

Grange Cinema ㉚

234 Kilburn High Road
30 July 1914 - 14 June 1975

O n its opening the Kilburn Grange Cinema was hailed not only as Britain's first super-cinema but also as one of the largest cinematograph theatres in Europe. On the corner of Kilburn High Road and Messina Avenue, the purpose-built Grange boasted seating for 2028, hugely overshadowing the Biograph Cinema (7) at 236 Kilburn High Road.

The Grange Cinema was designed by Edward A Stone, the architect who had produced plans for the nearby Maida Vale Picture Palace (25) opened 18 months before and who later designed the famous Astoria cinemas at Finsbury Park and Brixton. The Grange is one of a few surviving examples in Britain that display cinema design at its point of departure from theatre planning. Entirely stone-built, the cinema was in the Baroque style, witness the barrel-vaulted roof and the round top-lit foyer. Other distinctive features included an oval vestibule, a graceful staircase and a winter garden restaurant. The large original dome over its front entrance can still be seen.

The Grange's first feature film was the silent version of *She Stoops to Conquer*, well supported by a Keystone Cops short, with musical accompaniment provided by the cinema's organ. Front stalls were 1s, back stalls 1s 6d and circle seats 2s. All seats were tip-up and covered in old-gold plush. There were children's shows at 6d on Saturday mornings.

Two years after opening, the Grange had remodelled its entrance vestibule. During the early 1920s, the running of the cinema was taken over Scala/Provincial Cinematograph Theatres. In 1927 the proscenium was widened by the architect M K Matthews, a new organ chamber was built over the 10ft 6in stage and four new dressing rooms were inserted underneath for variety turns. The same year also saw operations taken over by Associated Provincial Picture Houses. During this period, the Grange successfully introduced a mixed cine-variety programme, films alternating with stage plays and comedy/novelty turns.

In February 1929 the cinema was taken over by Gaumont British Pictures, as was the nearby Maida Vale Picture House. During the early 1930s, a Western Electric sound system was installed. Despite being overshadowed by the arrival in 1937 of its mighty Kilburn neighbour the 4004-seat Gaumont State Cinema, the Grange continued to attract audiences and contributed admirably to the variety of cinema available in the Kilburn area at the time. The Grange managed to stay open for the duration of the Second World War.

By the 1960s many movie goers had been lured away by bingo and television and the Grange accordingly reduced its seating

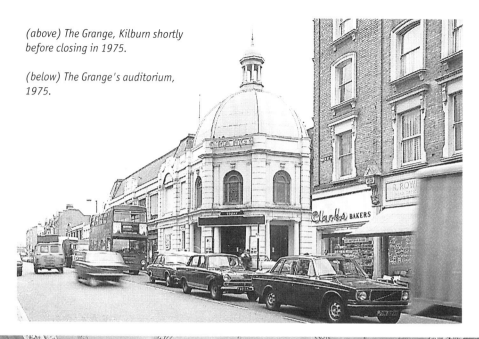

(above) The Grange, Kilburn shortly before closing in 1975.

(below) The Grange's auditorium, 1975.

capacity. The cinema closed on 14 June 1975. Its last programme was a British horror double bill, *The Ghoul* starring Peter Cushing and John Hurt, and *I Don't Want to be Born* with Joan Collins.

The building reopened on 23 February 1976 as Butty's Nightclub, going on to become the National Ballroom and then the National Club, a popular live music venue, often with an Irish flavour, as it is today. On 5 February 1991 the building received Grade II listing, on the same date as the Maida Vale Picture House.

II Inter-war period and the golden age of British cinema

Many of Camden's early cinemas closed during the First World War, and the 1920s saw fewer new cinemas opening. However, with the arrival of talkies in the late 1920s, interest in cinema revived. The next decade was hailed as the golden age of British cinema. Cinema buildings were bigger and more luxurious and, in Camden, these were no exception.

King's Cross Cinema   31
Gaumont, King's Cross
Odeon, King's Cross
Cineclub
King's Cross Cinema
Scala Cinema
275-277 Pentonville Road, N1
26 April 1920 - 6 June 1993

The purpose-built 1390 seat King's Cross Cinema designed by H Courtney Constantine was almost ready for use at the beginning of World War One, but a government ban on building places of amusement halted its completion. It was used during the war for the manufacture of aeroplane parts and later as a labour exchange for demobilised soldiers.

The premiere on 26 April 1920 was a veritable feast of celluloid entertainment. Lasting well over 3 hours and backed by a 20-piece orchestra, it included a panorama of beautiful coloured nature studies; Aston Villa winning the F A Cup; Vamps, Variety Artists And Models At Sea; Charlie Chaplin in *Hope Mission*, and finally *The Chinese Puzzle*, a mystery starring Leon M Lyons and Lillian Braithwaite. The building was 150ft long by 65ft wide and featured a 65ft high dome. Upon its 24ft by 18ft screen, performances were continuous. Admission ranged from 6d to 1s 9d, increasing at the top end to 3s in 1921 when the cinema was acquired by Tower (Rye Lane) Ltd.

By 1923 the King's Cross Cinema had become part of the Davis Circuit but on 21 December 1926 it was acquired by Associated Provincial Picture Houses who in turn, in February 1929, were take over by Gaumont British Pictures (GBP). As with other picture houses under its control, GBP staged free Christmas shows for local children at the cinema. For example, on the afternoon of 6 January 1933 nearly 1400 children were treated to a special film and variety presentation. In addition, each child received a free toy, chocolates, cakes and fruit. GBP were no doubt sowing the seeds in return for securing a future generation of film goers!

The cinema was closed after the Second World War in order to repair wartime damage. Now owned by Rank, it reopened as the Gaumont, King's Cross on 17 March 1952, having been completely refurbished by architects T P Bennett and Sons. In 1962 it became the Odeon. The building closed as a mainstream circuit picture house on 22 August 1970 after the last screening of *Airport*.

In February 1971 it resumed cinematic duties. Now known as the Cineclub, uncensored adult films were the order of the day. This policy was short-lived, and four months later the name reverted to the King's Cross Cinema and mainstream features returned, plus all-night rock concerts at weekends. During 1973 plans to convert the building into a pleasure palace with twin cinemas, a disco, bingo hall and amusement arcade were proposed but never realised. A few years later, on 12 April 1975, this

phase of the cinema's history was to end. Following a spaghetti western double-bill of *The Good, the Bad and the Ugly* and *A Fistful of Dollars,* the building closed.

The building remained dark for a while but in 1980 its new owners, Primatarium Ltd, reopened the auditorium as a Primatarium - an audiovisual ecology exhibition highlighting problems facing the world environment. The project was short-lived, and the building was converted into offices, with a snooker hall in the stalls area. On 9 July 1981 cinema returned, with a screening of the 1933 version of *King Kong*, when the Scala Cinema Club(48) transferred here from Tottenham Street and set up in the remaining circle area. As the Scala, it became one of London's best known repertory/ art house cinemas,

The former King's Cross Cinema as the Scala Cinema Club in 1982.

even though soundtracks had to compete with the rumble of underground trains below!

In 1993 the Scala Cinema Club went into receivership. Its last screening, on 6 June, was a Hong Kong gangster movie *Full Contact*. The closure came at the end of a number of well publicised events affecting the cinema. Prior to closing, the Scala's management lost a court case over an illegal screening of director Stanley Kubrick's banned film *A Clockwork Orange*. Although enough money was raised to pay a breach of copyright settlement, it was a tripling of rent upon renewal of lease that perhaps came as the final blow. Other factors may have contributed to the decision not to continue business, such as home video and a general blight affecting the King's Cross area. Currently the Scala building is being operated as a nightclub.

Victory ③²
Bloomsbury Cinema
Bloomsbury Super
114-118 Theobalds Road, WC1
3 September 1921 - November 1940

After an 8-year delay in opening due to First World War restrictions, the Victory cinema opened on 3 September 1921. Working with Ernest Mann's original plans, the architect responsible for completing the final design was Victor Peel. Situated on the corner of Theobalds Road and New North Street, Holborn, the building cost a reputed £85,000 and had seating for 1372. Living quarters were also incorporated into the design.

Mr James Rolls, the Lord Mayor of London, officiated at the Victory's opening ceremony and was later presented with a key enabling him to enter the cinema whenever he wished, presumably during performance time! The opening featured a special presentation of Charlie Chaplin's film *The Kid*, which was

VICTORY CINEMA,

THEOBALD'S ROAD, W.C. 1.

Resident Manager - Mr. Percy Marland.

GRAND OPENING ON SATURDAY, September 3, at 6 p.m.

This beautiful Super-Cinema has been built for Comfort and Clear Projection.

SPECIAL OPENING ATTRACTION,

CHARLIE CHAPLIN
AND
JACKIE COOGAN IN
" THE KID "

Orchestral Selections by

The Victory Symphony Orchestra of Twenty Performers.

PRICES OF ADMISSION
6d. to 2/. (plus tax).

'Phone MUSEUM 4278.

The Right Hon. Alderman JAMES ROLL, Lord Mayor,

accompanied by The Lady Mayoress and the Sheriffs will perform the opening ceremony at 3 p.m.

Opening advertisement for the Victory (Holborn Guardian, 2 September 1921).

screened to 300 soldiers before the cinema was given over to public performance. Performances were accompanied by the cinema's 20 piece symphony orchestra. Another attraction at the Victory was its American soda-fountain. A contemporary advert in the *Holborn Guardian* stated that the Victory was the only picture house in London which could boast "a ventilation plant which effectively kills influenza germs and purifies the air". Apparently the air conditioning system used the same principle as that once installed on London Underground Railways! Performances were continuous, with three programme changes weekly. Tickets cost between 6d and 2s and three-seater boxes were 3s per person.

By 1925, now under the control of Bloomsbury Cinemas Ltd, the cinema had been renamed the Bloomsbury. In November 1929 another takeover occurred, this time by London and Southern Cinemas Ltd, with change of name to the Bloomsbury Super. A year or so later the company installed a Western Electric Sound System.

Just before closure in November 1940, one last change in ownership occurred, to the Odeon group. The last films to be advertised at the Super, *Zaza* starring Claudette Colbert and *His Brother's Keeper* with Tamara Desin, appeared on 17 November. However, during the early hours of 11 May 1941, the cinema's closure was made permanent when the building suffered a direct hit from a parachute mine incendiary. The cinema was never rebuilt. Mercury House now stands on the site, home to Cable and Wireless Ltd.

The aftermath of an air raid on Holborn, May 1941. The remains of the Bloomsbury Super.

Tolmer

Tolmers Square, NW1
May 1924 - 22 March 1972

32

S ituated to the west of Euston Station, the Tolmer cinema gained a reputation for being one of the capital's most (in)famous flea-pits. It was also one of the cheapest. Even at the time of closure, seats were priced at the amazingly cheap 15p and 25p!

Proprietor George Smart, aided by manageress Mrs Hodges, opened the Tolmer to the public in May 1924. The building was perhaps the most unusual to have been converted to cinema use in the Camden area. It began life as the Tolmers Square Congregational Church dating back to 1863. In fact, four years after conversion, the building had its original spire still attached!

It is reported that it was finally removed around 1928/29. With a large seating capacity of 1050, early admission prices ranged between 6d and 1s 6d. The cinema presented daily continuous performances which changed three times weekly.

By 1941 A H Partridge had become trustee of the cinema but in 1944 the building was bought by the Pomson family trading as New Tolmer Ltd. After restoration following World War Two bomb damage, it was run as a family type cinema. Programmes were still changed three times per week and always contained double bills, most of which were second run features.

During the early 1970s the Tolmer had become extremely tatty and was in need of substantial repair to satisfy safety requirements. Meanwhile, the surrounding area of Tolmers Square had been ear-marked for major redevelopment. Following two

The Tolmer shortly after closing in 1972

43

TOLMER CINEMA

Monday, October 13th for 3 days

MAMIE VAN DOREN   LORI NELSON
UNTAMED YOUTH
At 3.15 6.10 9.5   (A)

JOHN AGAR   MARLA ENGLISH
FLESH AND THE SPUR
In Colour
At 1.45 4.35 7.30   (A)

Thursday, October 16th for 3 days

RANDOLPH SCOTT
7 MEN FROM NOW
In Colour
At 3.10 6.10 9.0   (U)

FERNANDEL
JOINS THE ARMY
At 1.30 4.30 7.25   (A)

SUNDAY, OCTOBER 19th one day only

TONY CURTIS
FORBIDDEN

AND

RICHARD FRASER
THE COBRA STRIKES
A)

NOTE THE PRICES 1/- & 1/6   CIRCLE 2/-

A varied programme from "your cheapest and best house of entertainment", the Tolmer. October 1958.

unsuccessful applications to rebuild the cinema as part of a hotel/office complex, the owners finally sold the building to property developers. Its last double-bill presentation of the aptly titled *Die Slowly, You'll Enjoy It More* and *The Looters* occurred on 22 March 1972, after which the Tolmer finally closed.

Not withstanding a much publicised fight by locals to save the square and its buildings from redevelopment, the Tolmer cinema and surrounding area were swept away and the proposed plan to build new housing and retail premises realised.

Kilburn Empire Music Hall ㉞
Essoldo
Classic
Broadway Cinema

9-11 The Parade, Kilburn High Road, NW6
6 November 1927 - 12 April 1981

Opening around 1906 as the Kilburn Empire Music Hall and Theatre of Varieties, throughout its history the building has indeed been a theatre of variety in the widest sense. Until its final demolition in 1994, the Empire has played host to a diverse catalogue of entertainment, ranging from music hall and variety, cinema and live drama to religious worship and even war games!

W G R Sprague was the architect responsible for the design of the 1,913 seat Kilburn Empire. The Empire was later renamed the Vaudeville Theatre but later reverted to its original name. For its first 20 years, although live acts formed the main attraction at the venue, films were regularly shown as part of the evening's entertainment. However, under the control of Greater London Cinema and Theatres Ltd, a licence was acquired to operate as a part-time cinema. Commencing Sunday, 6th November 1927, and each Sunday from 5.30pm onwards, "High Class" pictures would be shown continuously. Admission prices varied. Balcony seats were priced at 6d, whilst stall seats ranged from 9d, 1s 3d to 1s 6d. Most expensive were seats for the grand circle which were priced at 1s 10 and 2s 4d. Contrary to the belief that the theatre turned it's back on live variety, the Empire began to show these films only on Sundays, with live performances still taking place on weekdays.

By 1931 the Empire had been taken over by Metropolitan and Provincial Cinematograph Theatres Ltd and, by 1942, Kilburn Varieties had assumed running of the building. At this time, the Empire had re-established itself as a very popular wartime live variety theatre, presenting a mixture of light entertainment

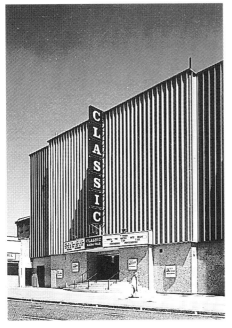

and theatrical drama. This policy continued after the war until 1948, when a year later the Empire finally opened as a fully fledged cinema, following extensive re-decoration and installation of new sound and projection apparatus.

The cinema, renamed Essoldo after the chain operating the building, opened to the public on 6 June 1949, with *Man on the Run* starring Derek Farr and *Always Another Dawn*, with future presentations to be screened from the ABC circuit. In almost a reversal of the Empire's decision to show films only on Sundays in late 1927, the new Essoldo was to operate as a cinema only from Monday to Saturday; the BBC were to broadcast their popular Variety Bandbox from the cinema on Sundays. Unlike the Kilburn State and Kilburn Grange(30), management decided not to host children's Saturday cinema.

During 1970 the cinema was substantially

The former Kilburn Empire as the Classic in 1973, its original Edwardian frontage replaced with a faceless metal grill.

The former Kilburn Empire as the Essoldo in 1969.

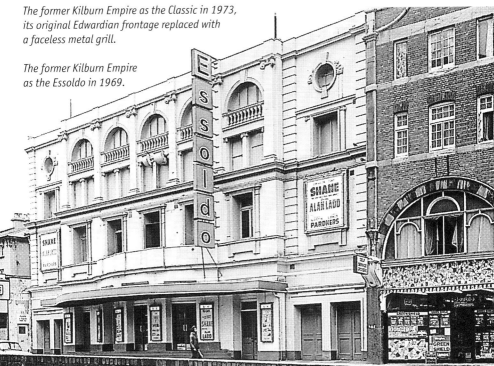

modernised, reducing the seating capacity to 471. It reopened on 3 December with the film *Catch 22*. Sadly, modernisation had completely eradicated the original facade of the Edwardian theatre. On 1 April 1972 the cinema became the Classic; this closed on 1 December 1973, reopened as the live Broadway Theatre but then reconverted to cinema as the Broadway Cinema, which staggered on through the 1970s showing a mixture of mainstream features as well a regular Asian language films. It finally closed on 12 April 1981 with the Kenyan film *Amin: The Rise and Fall.*

The 1980s saw the building used in a variety of ways. The World Renewal Spiritual Trust was given permission in 1984 to use it for public worship and recreational activities. By January 1990, a "paint-fight" war games experience had opened. However, in June 1994, the building was finally demolished. Today, the Regents Plaza, a luxury hotel, now dominates the site.

Dominion Theatre ㉟
269 Tottenham Court Road, W1
3 October 1929 - 1981

Opening as a live theatre on 3 October 1929, the theatre's entrance hall and foyer replaced the much smaller Court Cinema (19) which had recently closed. The rest of the Dominion was situated on part of the vast site of Meux's brewery. Designed by William and T R Millburn with an overall seating capacity of 2835, including 1340 seats in the stalls, 818 in the dress circle and 677 in an upper circle, the total cost was £459,727.

On 19 July 1930, Universal hired the theatre to show the UK film premiere of *Phantom of the Opera* starring Lon Chaney. The film included talking sequences with recorded sound effects and music. H G Wells was said to have been in the audience. The following year Charlie Chaplin's *City Lights,* also with music and effects, was screened, the star making a personal appearance.

Chaplin's film made a reappearance at the Dominion nearly 50 years later in a special revival screening! From January 1933, Associated Provincial Picture Houses began to operate the Dominion as a mostly second-run picture house, with live shows often accompanying films. In 1937, television was demonstrated at the theatre and 1938 saw the first display of colour television there.

The Dominion closed for the duration of the Blitz between October 1940 and January 1941. After the war, the theatre continued to show Gaumont releases but in the mid-1950s the owners, Rank, decided to reintroduce live acts and concerts, although films would continue when live events were not staged. In April 1957 the jazz and blues singer Sophie Tucker appeared and, according to the *Daily Express*, turned the cinema into "an American night-joint", a new role for the building! A few months later Judy Garland appeared in concert.

About this time the building received the new Todd AO film projection system, then the latest in film presentation technology. However, the 46ft screen and stereophonic sound reduced the seating capacity by over 1000. To make full use of this innovation, the management introduced, on 21 April 1958, the film version of *South Pacific* which began a record breaking run lasting over 4 years, playing 2551 times to over 3 million people and taking over £1.5 million. More long runs were to come: *Porgy and Bess, Cleopatra, The Sound of Music.* A month after this film closed in June 1968, the theatre was redecorated.

During the 1970s live events and feature films alternated, the former predominating by the early 1980s. Rank sold the theatre's lease in 1987 to a property company who then leased the building back on a short-term arrangement. The following year, the Dominion was granted Grade II listed status but, despite this, planning permission was sought to demolish the building and replace

Dominion Theatre, Tottenham Court Road in 1933.

47

it with a hotel and office complex. A request which, however, Camden Council refused.

Whether or not the theatre will ever screen films again remains to be seen. Ominously, its projection equipment and screen were removed in 1994. Today, under the proprietorship of Nederlander Dominion Ltd and operated by Apollo Leisure, the theatre continues to enjoy a successful run of live shows and musicals.

Regent Theatre ● 36
Century
Granada
37-43 Euston Road, NW1
26 December 1932 - 6 April 1968

Once situated on the corner of Euston Road and Tonbridge Street, on a site now covered by an extension of Camden Town Hall, the Regent Theatre cinema building started life as the Euston Palace of Varieties in 1900 to the designs of architects Bertie Crewe and Wylson and Long. Early theatre programmes show that films could be seen there regularly alongside live turns as part of an evening's entertainment before and during the First World War. With a change of name to the Regent Theatre in the early 1920s, the management concentrated on producing live plays, but by the 1930s the Regent had succumbed to the lure of cinema.

Under the proprietorship of King's Cross Cinemas Ltd, the theatre was reconstructed to the designs of Andrew Mather and opened as a cinema on 26 December 1932. With 1170 seats, the auditorium retained a number of early features, such as boxes with seats on either side of the screen, a reminder of its previous life as a music hall. A Western Electric Sound System was installed and the

(left) The Adventurers, a jungle thriller, showing at the Dominion in 1952.

(right) Regent Theatre, 1924. The building converted to cinema in December 1932.

theatre's cafe revamped. During its early years as a cinema, the Regent added live variety turns in support of the main feature. On 14 October 1935 the building was taken over by Associated British Cinemas (ABC), which a short time earlier had acquired other cinemas in the Camden area, namely the Forum(40) at Kentish Town and Camden Town's Bedford Theatre(37). The Regent was under the control of ABC until 24 December 1949, when an independent operator took over, to be succeeded in 1954 by the Granada Group, which renamed it the Century on 13 September that same year. Two years later old-time music hall and variety made a brief comeback when comedian Max Miller initiated proceedings and declared the building a live theatre once more. However, in 1958 the building returned to cinematic use.

The Century became the Granada on 6 May 1967, but its days as a picture house were numbered. Less than a year later, it closed after screening its last two features, *The Heroin Gang* and *The Eye of the Devil*.

On 1 May 1968, in an opening ceremony featuring singer Joe Brown, bingo was introduced but in 1969 the building closed for the last time. It was later demolished to make way for the extension to Camden Town Hall, officially opened in 1977.

An interior view of the Century (Regent Theatre) c.1963, showing its theatre boxes still in place either side of the screen.

Bedford Theatre

93-95 Camden High Street, NW1
1933 - 11 December 1939

The famous Bedford Theatre, situated in the heart of Camden Town and immortalised by artist Walter Sickert, was no stranger to film, having presented news reels and shorts as part of variety programmes as early as 1899. However, it became a full-time ABC cinema in 1933. By this time, the auditorium had been fitted with a new RCA Photophone Sound System. With 1259 seats and continuous daily performances (separate presentations shown on Sundays), admission prices in 1933 ranged between 4d and 1s 6d, rising to 1s 9d in 1936.

This former music hall and live theatre building was run as a cinema by ABC until 24 June 1939 and then independently on

The 1170 seat auditorium of the Century (Regent Theatre) c.1963.

behalf of the Bedford Music Hall Company until its final closure as a cinema on 11 December 1939. Its last film being *Keep Your Seats Please* starring George Formby. Two weeks later on Boxing Day the Bedford returned to live variety. Sadly, the building was demolished in 1968. Retail premises now cover where the theatre's original frontage stood, whilst residential accommodation (88 Arlington Road) erected by Community Housing Association and Bridge Housing now occupies the site of the auditorium.

Double bill at the Bedford (St Pancras Chronicle, 17 September 1937).

Everyman Cinema
Hollybush Vale, NW3
26 December 1933 - present

One of London's best-known film art-houses, and often labelled "the oldest repertory cinema in the world", Hampstead's Everyman Cinema celebrated its 60th anniversary as a cinematograph theatre during 1994. Before its opening as a cinema,

The Everyman Cinema, Hampstead in 1971.

a Wardour Street film salesman was reported to have given the Everyman a lifespan of only 6 weeks! Today, the cinema continues to implement, largely unaltered, the programming policy initially adopted. Run as a cinema club with a nominal membership fee, the policy on which its reputation has been built is to present the best of old and new features. Programmes are mainly centred around foreign films, seasons of specialist repertory or independent releases.

The building was erected in 1888 by public subscription as a community centre and assembly rooms, to commemorate 50 years of Queen Victoria's reign. The centre was known as the Hampstead Drill Hall and, as such, was the base for the volunteer Hampstead Regiment. However, by the late 1890s, the Drill Hall was reported to use its basement regularly to screen the new cinematograph sensation! Indeed, when it opened in 1933 as a fully fledged cinema, the auditorium was in the basement. Before this, the hall had opened as the Everyman Theatre on 15 November 1920, presenting innovative stage plays and launching new playwrights. However, by the early 1930s, the theatre was in financial difficulties and in November 1933 it closed. One month later the former Drill Hall became the Everyman Cinema Theatre.

Founded by local solicitor and film lover, James Fairfax-Jones, who stayed with the cinema until his death in 1974, the 245 seat Everyman opened to the public on 26 December 1933. Responsible for the adaptation of the cinema from a theatre was leading cinema architect Alistair MacDonald, son of Prime Minister Ramsay MacDonald. Mr Fairfax-Jones had gained earlier cinema experience when he formed a film society in Southampton, although on his arrival at the Everyman he found the theatre "dilapidated, derelict and down-and-out". However, money for the lease of the building was

The Everyman Cinema, Hampstead in 1996. The oldest repertory cinema in the world!

raised from friends who were issued with penny shares. Even on the opening day, together with the cinema's chief projectionist Tom Robinson, James Fairfax-Jones was on the cash desk, whilst his wife tore the tickets! Admission ranged from 1s to 3s 6d.

The first film shown was French director Rene Clair's *Le Million*, about an artist who had won the huge state lottery but who could not find his winning ticket! *Le Million* was later featured in a number of specialist seasons and was also screened to celebrate the Everyman's 30th anniversary. The first programme also featured *Turbulent Timber*, a Mack Sennett comedy, a Disney cartoon and the Paramount news. In addition, actor and Hampstead resident Sir Gerald Du Maurier officiated and gave a speech at the opening. Early policy was to present a series of different films to find out what the local cinema goers would like to see. Despite this market testing the early days were not a great success.

The turning point came in 1934 with the screening of *Der Traumende Mond*, which featured Elisabeth Bergner. At the time the actress was currently appearing on stage in the West End and this helped immensely in promoting the film. Its huge success proved that if the correct film was presented the audiences could be attracted. However, specialist foreign films forming the backbone of the Everyman's programme were in short supply. To counter this, the Everyman started its own business to import these films. One of them was Jean Vigo's *Zero de Conduite*, which had previously been banned in France. Again, this film scored a big hit with the critics and public alike.

Themed seasons were introduced and became commonplace. An early one was the first of many Marx Brothers programmes. Advance publicity postcards advertised future presentations; in 1937, 5000 people were on the cinema's mailing list. The postcards later blossomed into newspapers detailing forthcoming attractions. By the end of the 1930s, French films began to

dominate. But this domination was placed on hold when the cinema closed in September 1940 due to Second World War contingencies.

On 22 April 1943 the Everyman reopened under the temporary management of Vincent Beecham, a relative of music conductor Sir Thomas Beecham, with a double bill of Dorothy Lamour in *Typhoon* and Mary Martin in *The Great Victor Herbert*. After the war and the return of James Fairfax-Jones, the Everyman resumed the screening of European films. Ten years later the cinema itself was refurbished, with the installation of a new Cinemascope screen and refashioning of the foyer area to accommodate the small Foyer Art Gallery, under the guidance of Mrs Tessara Fairfax-Jones, exhibiting works by young artists including David Hockney and Barbara Hepworth. Later, Sunday morning concerts were introduced. However, during the late 1960s the cinema began to lose its audience and by the early 1970s the Everyman had become a shadow of its former self.

During its days in the wilderness, Margaret O'Brien came in as General Manager, having managed the Electric Cinema in Notting Hill, to turn the Everyman's fortunes around. In 1984 the building was again refurbished with the aid of grants from the Greater London Council, Channel 4 and the British Film Institute. The auditorium was redecorated and a Dolby Stereo Sound System installed. On 21 October 1986 the Everyman opened a cafe/restaurant in the cinema's basement which eventually became a popular meeting-place. During the 1980s the Everyman introduced a children's Saturday cinema club and occasional themed cine-variety presentations in which live concerts followed film shows.

In December 1993, only days before the Everyman Cinema's 60th birthday, the Fairfax-Jones family sold the cinema's lease to former Olympic athlete June Paul, although Camden Council still own the building. Today, the Everyman continues to implement its popular programming policy whilst upholding the honour of being the world's oldest repertory company.

Odeon, Haverstock Hill ❸❾

201 Haverstock Hill, NW3
29 September 1934 - 7 November 1940
13 December 1954 - 23 September 1972

Supported by a Walt Disney Silly Symphony cartoon, the film version of the musical *Chu Chin Chow* starring George Robey was the main attraction at the opening of the Haverstock Hill Odeon. The Duchess of Marlborough was the officiating dignitary, together with the Mayor of Hampstead, Walter Newman, who described the cinema as "an asset to the borough".

This was in an effort to calm the anxiety of the many local residents who believed the cinema would spoil the character of Hampstead and Belsize Park. However, the Odeon soon established itself as a popular part of the community's social life.

During construction of the building, to the plans of T P Bennett and Son, the cinema had been taken over by Oscar Deutsch, founder of the Odeon Cinema chain. Indeed, the Odeon at Haverstock Hill served as Deutsch's London flagship until he opened the Leicester Square Odeon in 1937. The Haverstock Hill Odeon contained many attractive features. The auditorium, with 652 seats in the stalls and 892 in the circle, was luxuriously decorated with cove lighting around the proscenium. Admission was between 1s and 3s 6d. There were earphone facilities for the hard of hearing and a British

Odeon, Haverstock Hill. Pictured here in 1936 when it was Odeon's London flagship.

Thomson-Houston Sound System. A Compton Organ with illuminated console was also installed, despite Oscar Deutsch's dislike of cinema organs which he believed added little to a film presentation.

Six years after opening, the Odeon became a casualty of the Second World War. The cinema closed on 7 November 1940 due to severe damage caused by a delayed-action bomb. The last film shown before the incident was Mickey Rooney in *Andy Hardy Meets a Debutante*. A local newspaper described the building after as "looking more like a ruined, ancient amphitheatre than a cinema". It was 1954 before the Odeon could reopen.

The cinema was refurbished by the Odeon's original architects, T P Bennett and Son. Under the aegis of the Rank Organisation, the cinema's gala reopening on 13 December 1954 was a glittering occasion. This time the Mayor, Emmanuel Snowman, remarked that it "wipes away another of the borough's war scars". Also present were film stars Diana Dors, Jack Warner and Donald Sinden, the last starring in the cinema's opening attraction, *Mad about Men*. This more than ably supported by the Jacques Tati classic *Monsieur Hulot's Holiday*.

By the early 1970s the freeholders of the site bought back the building's lease from the Rank Organisation because the cinema was not paying its way. Despite protests, the Odeon closed its doors for the last time in September 1972 after showing *Pulp* starring Michael Caine and *Pussy Cat I Love You*. The building was later demolished, being partially replaced by retail outlets and a new cinema, the Screen on the Hill(49), which opened in 1977.

The auditorium of the Odeon, Haverstock Hill with its Compton Organ centre stage, 1936.

Forum
ABC, Kentish Town

⓴

9-17 Highgate Road, NW5
17 December 1934 - 18 July 1970

"You will never leave this theatre without feeling that you have had your money's worth".

This quotation from entrepreneur Herbert Yapp, on the opening of his new Forum cinema in Kentish Town, appeared in the building's premiere brochure. Certainly Yapp, who also established Forum cinemas in London's Fulham Road and in Ealing, had spared little expense in producing this one.

Built during the golden years, the cinema was fitted with a Compton Organ (to be played initially by H J Downson) and a 5-ton safety curtain and had a seating capacity of 2175. It was designed by John Stanley Beard, who over 20 years earlier had designed Kentish Town's Palace cinema (28). His partner W R Bennett designed the interior. The proscenium was 35ft wide, the stage 25ft deep and there were six dressing rooms. On its exterior were quasi-Egyptian black columns set against a white background. There was a large first-floor tea lounge and dance hall where afternoon tea dances and evening supper dances were held. For the ladies, a special cosmetics room was incorporated into the design. Early admission prices ranged from 6d to 2s.

The cinema's opening was a lavish affair. To a fanfare of trumpets, the Forum was officially opened by stage and screen star Sydney Howard. Those present also enjoyed

The Forum, Kentish town taken shortly after opening. Today, the building is Grade II listed

a variety of film shorts and live music recitals before settling down to watch the cinema's main feature *The Church Mouse*, a comedy starring Laura La Plante and Ian Hunter.

A few months after this opening, in March 1935, the Forum and its sister cinemas were taken over by the ABC chain, although it was not until around 1963 that the cinema changed its name to the ABC, Kentish Town. After a double bill of *The Arrangement* and *Music*, the cinema closed in 1970. As with many former picture houses, the building became home to bingo and was later converted for ballroom use.

During the 1980s, the building was renamed the Town and Country Club, becoming an extremely popular live music venue. In 1991, the building was listed Grade II. A year later, it became the Forum once more, still playing host to live music and continues to do so today. In 1995, cinema returned briefly to the Forum when music films occasionally formed part of a Sunday night music and dance variety programme.

Paramount ●41
Odeon, Tottenham Court Road
Tottenham Court Road/Grafton Way, W1
10 February 1936 - 5 March 1960

"Time's magic wand", so the *St Pancras Chronicle* for 7 February 1936 reported, bought about the transformation of the site of the former Shoolbred's Department store in Tottenham Court Road into the Paramount. It took a little more than the

The opening programme for the Forum, Kentish Town. Officially opened by actor Sydney Howard.

PROGRAMME

PREMIER PERFORMANCE
MON., DEC. 17, 1934
AT 2.30 P.M.

1. **FANFARE OF TRUMPETS**
Trumpeters of His Majesty's Coldstream Guards

2. **OPENING CEREMONY**
by
MR. SYDNEY HOWARD
Supported by Mr. Herbert A. Yapp and Mr. J. Stanley Beard, F.R.I.B.A.

3. **THE NATIONAL ANTHEM**
Sung by **OLIVE GILBERT**

4. **VIEWS OF THE NEWS**
Pathe Super Sound Gazette

5. **FORUM IN THE MAKING**
See How It's Done

MR. SYDNEY HOWARD

6. **A MUSICAL COCKTAIL**
H. A. Dowson at the Compton Organ

7. **ALFREDO AND HIS FAMOUS GYPSY ORCHESTRA**

8. **FUTURE FILM FARE**

9. **OLIVE GILBERT**
The Famous Operatic Contralto—Carl Rosa Opera Co.

10. **LAURA LA PLANTE**
in
THE CHURCH MOUSE
Cert. A
with **IAN HUNTER**
Delightful Comedy Drama

11. **THE KING**

wave of a magic wand to create this impressive cinema. Built at a reported cost of £108,000, its construction is said to have employed 1000 men working for 5 months and incorporated 950 tons of steel, 1500 tons of cement and 2000 gallons of paint! Responsible for the design were Frank Verity and Samuel Beverley. Featuring a huge 2568 seat auditorium (to be reduced by 700 seats a little over 20 years later), it was decorated in marine green, Italian blue and Chinese orange. The building included a cafe/restaurant over its rounded corner entrance and a dance hall. The proscenium was 55ft wide, the stage 25ft deep and there were twelve dressing rooms.

Performing the opening ceremony was the Mayor of St Pancras, F W Fincham, all proceeds of the night's taking being donated to the University College Hospital extension fund. Also present were film stars Maurice Chevalier and Anna Neagle with her film producer husband Herbert Wilcox. The

Paramount's first features were *Millions in the Air* and *The Return of Peter Grimm,* both films receiving their European premieres. The two films were accompanied by a spectacular stage show entitled *Dazzle,* which featured various acts involving 76 artists. These included members of the Paramount Orchestra, the Paramount Tiller Girls and organist Mr Reginald Foort recruited from the Paramount Theatre, New York. Subsequent film presentations were also fully supported by the Paramount Stage Show. Programmes changed every Sunday, with admission prices ranging between 9d and 1s 6d for matinees and 1s to 2s 6d for evening performances.

In November 1946 the cinema became the

(below) Paramount, Tottenham Court Road taken a week after opening in 1936.

(right) Coming alive at night. The Paramount in 1938.

Odeon, following a takeover by the Odeon Group some four years earlier. Although not publicly introduced until later, in 1953 the cinema hosted the first British demonstration of Cinemascope. In 1958, the Odeon introduced another large-screen system,

Cinemiracle, which proved short-lived. But the Paramount's days were numbered. It closed on 5 March 1960 with a screening of a Cinemascope picture, *The Story on Page One* starring Rita Hayworth. Its decline could perhaps be attributed to its distance from

the West End, as well as the decline in local population.

More saddening is the fact that, following demolition, the site was not developed and today still remains empty, the victim of Health Authority planning blight (it belongs to University College Hospital), having served as a car park for many years. Advertising boards conceal the site from public view. Memory of the cinema lingers on in Paramount Court, a residential block located nearby in University Street.

Gaumont, Regent's Park ㊷
Odeon, Camden Town
Gate 3
Parkway Cinema(s)
14 Parkway, NW1
25 January 1937 - 23 August 1993

omedian Will Hay and actress Lilli Palmer were the guests of honour at the gala opening of the Gaumont, Regent's Park on 25 January 1937. As one of the major picture houses in the Gaumont British Picture Corporation, with a seating capacity of 2742, the Gaumont soon established itself as one of North London's finest cinemas, but then experienced varied fortunes. Falling foul of dwindling audiences and partial conversion to bingo during the 1960s, the Gaumont enjoyed a return to former glory in the 1980s as the Parkway Cinema under the management of Peter Walker. Then, amidst bitter controversy, the cinema closed in August 1993. Current plans are to reopen the building as a multi-screen Odeon cinema in 1997.

The Gaumont was built for Provincial Cinematograph Theatres, a subsidiary of Gaumont British, and designed by architects

W E and Sydney Trent and Daniel McKay. It took nearly 12 months to complete and, according to the local press, employed 200 St Pancras labourers. The stage alone cost £10,000 and housed a Compton Organ built at the Willesden works of John Compton. The organ console appeared to the side of the stage instead of the usual central position. The interior was both luxurious and stylishly comfortable with ornate plaster work, hardwood panelling and tasteful lighting. The auditorium featured a proscenium 44ft wide, a 31ft deep stage, twelve dressing rooms and one bathroom. Also incorporated was a lavish entrance foyer and circle lounge area, as well as a first-floor cafe restaurant.

The Gaumont was opened by St Pancras Mayor F W Fincham. The opening feature was *Showboat* starring Paul Robeson and was supported by *The Two Fisted Gentleman* with James Dunn. Also on the bill for the day was a Mickey Mouse short, Terance Casey at the Compton Organ and the GB Revels in a spectacular stage show! Admission prices depended on the time and day of a performance. Prices for matinee performances between 12pm and 3.30pm were 6d, 1s and 1s 6d, whilst performances after 3.30pm and all day Sundays were 9d, 1s 4d, 2s and 2s 6d. For children, the cinema established a Saturday morning Kiddies Club with admission at 3d. At the first meeting of the club a live penguin from London Zoo was introduced as mascot to the Saturday morning shows, with children later being asked to choose a suitable name for the bird. The result unfortunately not recorded.

The Gaumont enjoyed a successful run during the 1940s and 1950s, with concerts given by named stars being a feature during the latter decade. Amongst those who performed were Bob Hope and orchestra leader Mantovani. On 30 May 1964, the Gaumont became an Odeon Cinema. Soon afterwards the cinema was deemed too large for the dwindling audiences and between November 1967 and February 1968 the entire stalls area became home to the Top Rank Bingo Club entered from Arlington Road. The cinema's circle area became its auditorium with a seating capacity of only 1198. When in the early 1990s application was made for Grade II listing this failed because the 1960s restructuring had been so extensive.

The Odeon survived the 1960s and most of the 1970s, despite decreasing attendances at cinemas generally. The last screening before closure on 29 September 1979 featured Joan Collins in *The Bitch*. The cinema lay empty for over a year until it was reopened on 9 October 1980 as Gate 3 by the independent

(left) Gaumont, Regent's Park in 1937.

(centre) Gate 3 cinema in 1982. Formerly the Gaumont, it later became the Parkway.

(right) The former Gaumont, Regent's Park as the Parkway Cinema in 1992.

61

Cinegate Company with a previously lost 1923 Charlie Chaplin film, *A Woman of Paris*. Seating capacity was now down to 424 seats. Gate 3 enjoyed a short run of success screening independent, less commercial mainstream first runs and repertory features. Nevertheless, the building closed once again on 19th July, 1982.

15 December 1983 inaugurated the period of flamboyant management under Peter Walker, with a showing of Sean Connery as Bond in *Never Say Never Again*. Becoming the Parkway Cinema, its seating capacity had been restored to 1000, and much of the luxury of the original Gaumont had been recreated: the entrance foyer and staircase, and the first-floor lounge, were refurbished.

Free cinema shows for children and senior citizens were regular events and, as a result, the Parkway became an important social focal point for the local community.

A second screen was added in the former Gaumont's tea lounge. Named the Regency, this 90-seat auditorium opened on 17 May 1985 with *Amadeus*. Its larger sister was named the King's, and the building was now called the Parkway Cinemas. In 1986, because of the Parkway's success, Peter Walker received a BFI award for "injecting much-needed individualism into cinema exhibition". However, the following year the cinema's lease expired, and the leaseholders Rank did not renew, as they intended to convert to a multi-screen complex, with total

Gaumont's auditorium in 1937, holding a capacity of 2742.

restructuring. Despite local demonstrations and campaigns and Camden Council's refusal to give Rank planning permission to redevelop the site, the building closed on 2 March 1987.

For the next few years the cinema was dark, but the Parkway reopened on 14 December 1989, once again under Peter Walker's management, his renewal of lease finally granted. The reopening ceremony featured a marching band and chamber orchestra followed by the Parkway's opening film, Disney's cartoon feature *Oliver and Co*. The smaller Regency screen reopened a little later on 9 February 1990. The development company, Bernard Sunley and Sons, had bought the cinema's freehold with an

agreement to put the cinema back into the hands of Peter Walker. However, plans later surfaced showing that the company wanted to re-vamp the cinema and its surrounding site as part of an £80 million redevelopment scheme. Meanwhile, Peter Walker had continued his policy of special screenings, subsidised rates for senior citizens and generally promoted the idea of "bringing the West End to Camden Town".

By early 1993 history repeated itself as Peter Walker's 3 year lease was not to be renewed and plans were launched to develop the site. However, planning permission for redevelopment was rejected by Camden Council, on the grounds that the proposed new building would disfigure the Camden

A return to cinema's golden age. The Parkway's Art-Deco style entrance foyer, 1992.

Town Conservation area. Sadly though, following notices to quit, and later legal proceedings against Mr Walker, the Parkway Cinema finally closed on 23 August 1993, in spite of a hugely successful run of the cinema's last feature, the record-breaking *Jurassic Park*. Since its closure, negotiations between the owners, Camden Council and the Friends of Parkway Cinema to reopen the building have taken place, but with little success. In an additional sad blow for Camden Town, and leaving the area without a local cinema, the Parkway's neighbouring cinema, the Plaza(2), was also closed little over a year later (29 September 1994) following repossession of the building by owners, Bernard Sunley Ltd.

In 1995 Rank planned to convert the Parkway Cinema into a multiplex Odeon. Local campaigners were and are still worried that parts of the building's interior decor, as well as the cinema's main auditorium, will be lost in reconstruction. For brief periods during 1995 and 1996 squatters acted as impromptu caretakers of the building, even managing to screen a few films and offered free seats to passers by! However, January 1997 saw Odeon Cinemas buy the building from the owners, followed by an application to Camden Council for a cinema licence. It is envisaged that a five screen multi-plex will open on the site in 1997 but, according to the local press, it is believed that none of the Parkway's grand architectural features will remain. Nevertheless, when the doors of the former Gaumont open once again and cinema returns to Camden Town another chapter in the building's cinematic history will begin!

The Parkway's refurbished first floor lounge, 1992.

Odeon, Swiss Cottage (43)

96 Finchley Road, NW3
4 September 1937 - present

Originally, Robert Cromie's plans for a new Finchley Road cinema for the Eldorado Cinematograph Company were drawn up in 1935. However, under the direction of Harry Weedon and his staff, the designs were later realised for the Odeon Company and the cinema opened on 4 September 1937.

Situated on an island site adjacent to the famous Swiss Cottage public house, the Odeon incorporated 2115 seats, 1281 in the stalls and 834 in the circle. The auditorium also featured a 3/8 Compton Theatre Organ with Melotone and Grand Piano and illuminated console, not removed until 1964.

The Odeon's official opening by the Mayor of Hampstead, Dr Lewis Glover, was a grand occasion. Guests included Oscar Deutsch (founder of the Odeon Chain), architect Harry Weedon, Alexander Korda and the Maharajah of Jaipur. The crowds waiting outside were also pleased to see film stars Merle Oberon and Conrad Veidt. Proceeds of the opening gala went to the Swiss Cottage School for the Blind and the Hampstead Children's Hospital. The opening feature was the British film *Farewell Again* starring Flora Robson and Leslie Banks. After the film, guests danced on the stage until after midnight!

From May 1964, the Odeon also became home to weekly musical events. During the 1960s the Royal Philharmonic Orchestra gave Sunday evening concerts through to

Odeon, Swiss Cottage in 1937.

November 1967. On 25 February 1973, the cinema became the thirteenth Rank cinema to convert to the multi-screen approach first introduced 8 years earlier in Nottingham. The three-screen Odeon was opened by Camden's Mayor, Brian Duggan, who ceremoniously snipped a length of cinematograph film to open the 780 seat Screen 1, the gold-coloured 109 seat Screen 2 and the turquoise 105 seat Screen 3. Although conversion cost £35,000, with the original seating capacity halved, prices at the new-look Odeon remained unchanged. Entrance to Screen 1 was 40p, 45p and 50p, whilst admission to Screens 2 and 3 was 60p, with children under 14 at half price and pensioners 5p for all performances. The first films shown at the new look Odeon were *The Ragman's Daughter*,

Fiddler on the Roof and *Hammersmith is Out.*

The conversion to a triple screen, none-theless, nearly had disastrous consequences in 1986 when a proposed new development threatened to demolish the Odeon to make way for a new centre, featuring a block of flats, a smaller cinema, a local studies centre, and other amenities. It was reported that Rank considered the cinema not worth saving, as the interior had been spoiled by the earlier triple-screen conversion! However, the redevelopment scheme was eventually abandoned.

Six years later the Odeon doubled its screen capacity. Upon unveiling a commemorative plaque and cutting an "O" for Odeon shaped cake, Hampstead and Highgate MP Glenda Jackson officially

The Swiss Cottage Odeon's 2115 seat auditorium, 1937. Its Compton Organ was removed in 1964.

opened the cinema's new £600,000 six-screen conversion on 5 September 1992. The gala ceremony to mark the occasion saw a premiere screening of the Australian smash hit film *Strictly Ballroom*, supported by a live performance by Ballroom Dance Champions. The conversion had taken over four months to complete, during which the cinema stayed operational by keeping one screen open at a time. The Odeon now comprises one 686 seat auditorium, one of 250, one of 150, one of 153, one of 120 and one of 112 seats, a total of 1471 seats.

Today, the Odeon, Swiss Cottage remains one of four cinemas open in the Hampstead area of Camden. However, if plans proceed, these may be joined by a fifth in December 1998 when a 2000 seat, 8-screen Warner

Brothers multi-plex is due to open in Finchley Road as a part of a huge shopping development. The arrival of the new cinema complex may of course have an influential effect upon the future of its Finchley Road neighbour but for the present, together with the ABC(26) at Pond Street, the Odeon cinema will continue to provide the area's popular, mainstream film entertainment.

Embassy   ⓸⓸
194 Tottenham Court Road, W1
25 September 1939 - 14/15 October 1940

An early Second World War casualty, this short-lived Tottenham Court Road cinema was badly damaged by an air

Luxurious comfort at the Swiss Cottage Odeon's first floor lounge, 1937.

raid on the night of 14/15 October 1940. As a result, the cinema was never to reopen. Having closed temporarily at the height of the Blitz in September 1940, the Embassy had enjoyed only one year's service since opening on 25 September 1939.

Built at a modest cost of £45,000, this 782 seat cinema was designed by Montague Cohen and Arnold Michaels on a site vacated by Heal's furniture store, which had moved next door. Initially screening mainly foreign-language films, the cinema later changed its programming policy to include Hollywood second-run and transfer features. Although remnants of the derelict cinema remained until the 1950s, its site was later reclaimed by Heal's as an extension to its store.

The Embassy (to the left of Heals)
a number of years after closing.
This view taken 1957.

III Post Second World War to present day

The years after the Second World War were not kind to cinema. 1946 witnessed an increase in cinema admissions but shortly after that, audience figures slowly began to fall. During the 1950s, this was attributed to competition from television, bingo and other activities. People's standards of living increased, homes became more comfortable and the need to escape to the picture house lessened.

The decline continued into the early 1980s. Many of Camden's early cinemas had long since closed, and only a handful of pre-World War Two picture houses and a few later additions survived, although Camden did see the opening of five cinemas during the 1970s. The mid 1980s witnessed an upturn in audience figures, but during this period only two new cinemas opened in the area. Despite the increase in interest in film into the 1990s, three of Camden's most famous cinemas had closed by 1994. There are plans in 1997 to convert one of these, the Parkway, into a multi-screen Odeon and proposals have been forwarded that may see the opening of a Warner Brothers multi-plex, Finchley Road in 1998.

at reduced prices. Admission was 4s and 6s, with 1s for OAPs at any time. Towards the end of its opening year, the cinema was also hired by film buffs to present late-night film shows. Before and after performances of such films as *The Bicycle Thieves,* the audience were encouraged to meet and discuss the presentation.

During the summer of 1971, Contemporary Films Ltd, who also ran the Paris Pullman cinema in Kensington, acquired the Venus in order to present first-run offbeat films. It is uncertain exactly when the Venus stopped operating: despite a threat of closure during 1972, the cinema ran for a few more years but it had closed by 1975. Its final demise marked the closure of the last cinema to operate in the Kentish Town area, which had once been home to eight cinemas. Although no films are presented commercially, the Venus's former home, St Andrew's Church Hall, is still in place today.

Venus   ㊺
Kentish Town Road, NW5
June/July 1970 - 1975

The Venus was a small cinema located on the ground floor of a modern church hall. Situated behind St Andrew's Greek Orthodox Church, itself located on the corner of Kentish Town Road and Rochester Road, the Venus was initially operated by Aphrodite Films. The air-conditioned 185 seat cinema, with licensed bar, opened in June/July 1970, offering mainstream second-run features

Kentish Town's Venus cinema, 1970.

ABC, Shaftesbury Avenue 46
Cannon, Shaftesbury Avenue
MGM, Shaftesbury Avenue
ABC, Shaftesbury Avenue
135 Shaftesbury Avenue, WC2
21 December 1970 - present

This cinema was originally designed by T P Bennett and Sons and opened in 1931 as the Saville Theatre. Owners of the new ABC circuit, EMI, reopened the Saville as the ABC 1 & 2 on 21 December 1970 with a gala event. At a conversion cost of £600,000, the interior was redesigned by William Ryder and Associates, who turned the theatre's original seating capacity of 1200 into two auditoriums, ABC 1 with 616 seats and ABC 2 seating 581. However, this refurbishment did not affect the building's exterior, and its original plaques representing Art through the Ages and a 130-ft frieze Drama through the Ages by Gilbert Bayes can still be seen on the cinema's frontage.

There's a Girl in my Soup opened ABC 1, whilst The Railway Children appeared in ABC 2. During 1986, the Cannon Group took over the ABC circuit and changed the cinema's name on 17 October to the Cannon. On 6 March 1992, after Cannon's parent company Pathe had acquired MGM/UA, the name changed again to MGM. In 1995, Richard Branson's Virgin Group took over a number of MGM cinemas, including this one but in June 1996 the group sold its interest in this and other MGM cinemas to a resurrected ABC Group. In consequence, and a little over 25 years after it opened, the cinema regained the name ABC, Shaftesbury Avenue. The cinema today continues to present first-run features.

MGM, Shaftesbury Avenue pictured here in early 1996. It became the ABC for the second time in June 1996 after a company take-over.

Bloomsbury Cinema
ABC Bloomsbury
EMI International
Film Theatre
Gate 2
Gate Bloomsbury 1 & 2
Renoir

Brunswick Centre, Brunswick Square, WC1
19 January 1972 - present

Built below ground level at a cost of £300,000, the 490 seat Bloomsbury Cinema was constructed as part of the Brunswick Centre housing and shopping development. Opening on 19 January 1972 with the film *The Trojan Women*, the Bloomsbury was the brainchild of American entrepreneur Walter Reade, who had built up a business in the USA importing highbrow foreign films which formed the basis of the cinema's initial programmes.

The Bloomsbury was not an immediate success. On 4 May 1974, under Lord Delfont, EMI took over and it became the ABC, Bloomsbury presenting films of more mainstream character. In January 1977, EMI renamed the cinema the EMI International Film Theatre to mark the return to the screening of foreign and independent features but within a month the company rented the building to Cinegate who were successfully operating the Gate cinema in Notting Hill. Consequently, the Brunswick Centre cinema became the Gate Two, Derek Jarman's *Jubilee* being its opening film.

The cinema was later converted into two auditoriums becoming now known as the Gate Bloomsbury 1 and 2 with a seating capacity of 251 and 241, respectively. This new incarnation was relatively short-lived and on 30 October 1985, following screening of *The Outcasts* and *The Shooting Party*, Cinegate closed the twin-screen cinema. EMI then leased the Gate, Bloomsbury to another

Renoir, Brunswick Square in 1996.

independent company, film distributor Artificial Eye, which had built up a solid reputation running similar venues, including the Plaza (2) in Camden Town.

With a 7-week and £80,000 facelift conducted by architects Burrell Foley Associates, who also designed the Metro Cinema in Piccadilly, Artificial Eye reopened the cinema as the Renoir (after the French film director) on 9 May 1986. The Renoir was launched with Agnes Varda's winner at the Venice Film Festival *Vagabond* and Alan Bleasdale's *No Surrender*. The cinema is today continuing a successful programming formula of mixing new foreign language and independent films with restored classics.

Scala Cinema Club, Tottenham Street in 1980/81. The club left the site in 1981 to relocate in King's Cross.

Other Cinema ⑱
Scala Cinema Club
25 Tottenham Street, W1
15 October 1976 - 1981

Opening on the site of the former Scala Theatre(15) under the guidance of one its founding members Nick Hart-Williams, the Other Cinema with its 330 seat basement auditorium began screening repertory and non-commercial/independent feature films on 15 October 1976. Its existence was, however, extremely short-lived and it closed on 15 February 1977. The auditorium was opened up again for cinematic use when the Scala Cinema Club screened its first programme on 1 June 1978. Although still presenting mostly repertory, this club tended to screen less avant-garde films than its predecessor.

The Scala Cinema Club left this address and

relocated to King's Cross in 1981. The Tottenham Street site was redeveloped and later became headquarters for the new Channel Four television company. Currently, another television company, Channel One Cable now occupies the premises.

Screen On The Hill   49
203 Haverstock Hill, NW3
9 November 1977 - present

One of London's most popular independent cinemas is located in the heart of leafy, residential Belsize Park. Behind the launching of the Screen On The Hill was Mainline Pictures, under the guidance of independent film entrepreneur Romaine Hart.

Built partly on the site of the Haverstock Hill Odeon (39), the Screen's comfortable auditorium seated 339. The seats were

exclusively supplied by Quinette of Paris. The cinema's opening film was American director Alan Rudolph's *Welcome to LA,* starring Keith Carradine. It was not long before the Screen established a reputation for presenting high-quality independent and specialist films.

In March 1983 the cinema launched a Saturday kids' club, with the help of local resident Tom Maschler, chairman of publishers Jonathan Cape. The first show, presided over by celebrity Nanette Newman, featured the film *The Black Stallion*, as well as a guest appearance by actor/writer Michael Palin and free ice cream! The following Saturday saw a guest appearance by Roald Dahl. This policy of providing Saturday club members with a mix of film and live "turns" proved a successful formula for some time.

In 1986, together with Parkway Cinema's (42) manager, Peter Walker, Romaine Hart won a BFI award for "injecting much-needed individualism into cinema exhibition". More recently the Screen On The Hill has received a facelift, and in October 1995, unveiled a new foyer featuring frosted mirrors, alpine green walls and a matching granite-trimmed coffee bar. The Screen continues to present quality, independent and specialist films, complementing those of the nearby Everyman (38).

Screen on the Hill, 1996. This popular independent cinema opened to the public in 1977.

Classic,
Tottenham Court Road
Cannon,
Tottenham Court Road
MGM, Tottenham Court Road
ABC, Tottenham Court Road
30 Tottenham Court Road, W1
30 July 1981 - present

50

The ceremonial cutting of a piece of 70mm film by Camden Mayor, Maureen Robinson, accompanied by a fanfare from trumpeters of the Welsh Guards, marked the opening of this, the Classic Group's 70th cinema to join its chain. Located partly on the site once occupied by three earlier cinemas, namely the Grand Central (11), the Carlton (27) and the Majestic Picturedrome (23), this triple screen complex seats 328 in Screen 1, 145 in Screen 2 and 137 seats in Screen 3.

The Classic's opening films featured *Condorman*,(a sports car used in the film added an attraction to the opening ceremony), *SOB* and *The Great Muppet Caper.* The last featured Miss Piggy from the Muppets who delivered a singing telegram as part of the ceremonies. Screen 1 usually presents mainstream features, while the other two screens present more varied foreign and independent releases. The cinema's exterior has a large neon display adjacent to its entrance which underneath shows a large view representing an audience.

From 6 December 1985 the complex became a Cannon cinema and in 1991, as with other cinemas in this group, it became an MGM cinema. June 1996 witnessed MGM

owners, Virgin, sell off many of their former MGMs, including this one, to a newly resurrected ABC company. Now renamed as such, it is the only cinema in Tottenham Court Road which in its history has contained no fewer than ten cinemas.

(left) Pictured here in 1996 as an MGM, this 3 screen cinema has since been renamed the ABC.

(below) Curzon Phoenix, 1996. One of Camden's three West End cinemas, the 212 seat building opened in 1987.

Curzon Phoenix

Phoenix Street, Charing Cross Road, WC2
20 March 1987 - present

This is one of Camden's three remaining central London cinemas. The 212 seat Curzon Phoenix reportedly cost £700,000. Its first presentation was the acclaimed Russian film *Come and See.* Built on a former car park, the cinema has no formal frontage or entrance and access to the auditorium is through the foyer of the neighbouring Phoenix Theatre. Films shown at the cinema are generally first-run features transferred from sister cinemas, Curzon West End in Shaftesbury Avenue and the Curzon Mayfair.

The cinemas of Camden:
a chronological list and map

1 **Dara**
   Delancey Street
   1908-1917
2 **Electric Theatre**
   Camden High Street
   1909-1994
3 **Kilburn Picture Palace**
   Belsize Road
   1909-1940
4 **Euston Cinema**
   Euston ROad
   1909-1940
5 **Eldorado**
   Heath Street
   1909-1916
6 **Gaiety**
   Tottenham Courtt Road
   1909-1940
7 **Biograph Theatre**
   Kilburn High Road
   1910-1917
8 **Gale Cinematograph Hall**
   Euston Road
   1910-1914
9 **Gem Picture Hall**
   Malden Road
   1910-1958
10 **Kentish Town Cinema**
   Gaisford Street
   1910-1960
11 **Grand Central**
   Tottenham Court Road
   1910-1931,
   1969-76
12 **Kilburn Electric Palace**
   Kilburn High Road
   1910-1916
13 **Holborn Cinema**
   High Holborn
   1910-1925
14 **Corner Theatre**
   Tottenham Court Road
   1910-1929
15 **Scala Theatre**
   Tottenham Sreett
   1911-1913
16 **Electric Alhambra**
   Kentish Town Road
   1911-1918
17 **Frognal Bijou Picture**
   House, Finchley Road
   1911-1931
18 **Coronation Gdns Cinema**
   Prince of Wales Road
   1911-1913
19 **Court Playhouse Cinema**
   Tottenham Court Road
   1911-1928

20 **Fitzroy Picture Palace**
   Charlotte Street
   1912-1916
21 **Electric Palladium**
   Camden High Street
   1912-1927
22 **Avenue Picture Palace**
   Pratt Street
   1912-1915
23 **Majestic Picturedrome**
   Tottenham Court Road
   1912-1976
24 **Camden Hippodrome**
   1a Camden High Street
   1913-1940
25 **Maida Vale Picture Palace**
   Maida Vale
   1913-1940
26 **Hampstead Picture Playhouse**
   Pond Street
   1913-present
27 **Carlton**
   Tottenham Court Road
   1913-1976
28 **Palace,**
   Kentish Town Road
   1913-1959
29 **Lismore**
   Lismore Road
   1914-1917
30 **Grange Cinema**
   Kilburn High Road
   1914-1975
31 **King's Cross Cinema**
   Pentonville Road
   1920-1993
32 **Victory**
   Theobald's Road
   1921-1940
33 **Tolmer**
   Tolmers Square
   1924-1972
34 **Kilburn Empire**
   Kilburn High Road
   1927-1981
35 **Dominion Theatre**
   Tottenham Court Road
   1929-1981
36 **Regent Theatre**
   Euston Road
   1932-1968
37 **Bedford Theatre**
   Camden High Street
   1933-1939
38 **Everyman Cinema**
   Hollybush Vale
   1933-present

39 **Odeon**
   Haverstock Hill
   1931-1940,
   1954-72
40 **Forum**
   Highgate Road
   1934-1970
41 **Paramount**
   Tottenham Court Road
   1936-1960
42 **Gaumont**
   Regent's Park,
   Parkway
   1937-1993
43 **Odeon Swiss Cottage**
   Finchley Road
   1937-present
44 **Embassy**
   Tottenham Court Road
   1939-1940
45 **Venus**
   Kentish Town Road
   1970-1975
46 **ABC**
   Shaftesbury Avenue
   1970-present
47 **Bloomsbury Cinema**
   Brunswick Square
   1972-present
48 **Other Cinema**
   Tottenham Street
   1976-1981
49 **Screen on the Hill**
   Haverstock Hill
   1977-present
50 **Classic**
   Tottenham Court Road
   1981-present
51 **Curzon Phoenix**
   Charing Cross Road
   1987-present

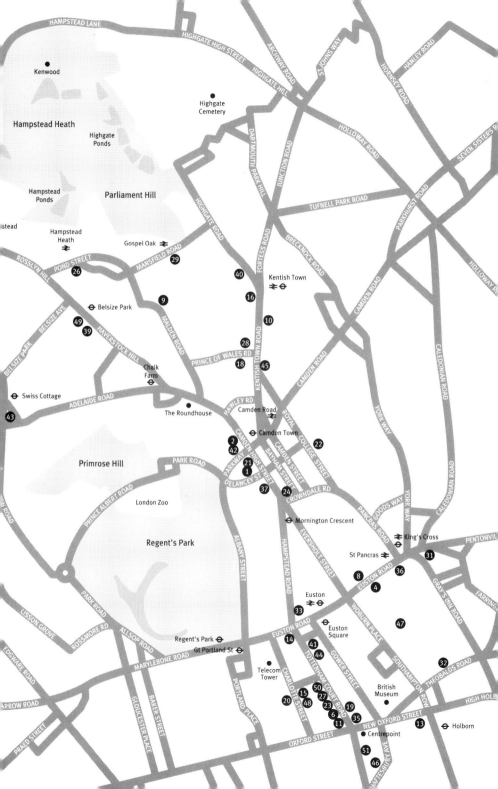

References and further reading

Barnes, John. The Rise of the Cinema in Britain, volume 2; Jubilee Year 1897. Bishopsgate Press, 1983.

Brooke, Michael et al. Everyman Cinema: 60th Anniversary Booklet. Everyman Cinema, 1994.

Clegg, Rosemary (ed). Odeon. Mercia Cinema Society, 1985.

Draper, Chris. Islington Cinemas and Film Studios. Islington Libraries, 1990.

Eyles, Allen and Skone, Keith. London's West End Cinemas. Keytone Publications, 1991.

Eyles, Allen. ABC: the First Name in Entertainment. Cinema Theatre Association/BFI, 1993.

Eyles, Allen. British Gaumont Cinemas. Cinema Theatre Assoc./BFI, 1996.

Fairfax-Jones, James. Running the Everyman. Sight and Sound Journal, Autumn 1937.

Howard, Diana. London Theatres and Music Halls 1850-1950. Library Association, 1970.

Howden, Peter. How to run a Cinema: an interview with Margaret O'Brien. Picture House no.20 Winter 1995/96. Cinema Theatre Association, 1995.

Jackson-Wrigley, M & Leyland, E. The Cinema. Grafton and Co, 1939.

Leigh, Mary. Merry-go-round. The Heathside Book Of Hampstead and Highgate. Edited by I Norrie. High Hill Press, 1962.

Sharp, Dennis. The Picture Palace. Hugh Evelyn Ltd, 1969.

Wates, Nick. The Battle for Tolmers Square. Routledge and Kegan Paul, 1976.

Webb, Malcolm. The Amber Valley Gazeteer of Greater London Suburban Cinemas 1946 - 1986. Amber Valley, 1986.

Index to cinemas